THE ULTIMATE VICTORIANS

This tasteful Italianate house in Alameda was the birthplace in 1873 of Joseph Knowland, Oakland *Tribune* publisher and United States Congressman and father of Senator William F. Knowland. When the Knowland house was built, Alameda was still an unincorporated township, a pastoral community of scattered estates called ranches, each with its own well and windmill, vegetable garden, orchards, cows and horses; some even had their own burial ground. One old-timer remembered the peninsula as being so densely wooded "you could hardly see the stars at night."

The
ULTIMATE VICTORIANS

of the continental side of San Francisco Bay

By Elinor Richey

BERKELEY · Howell-North Books · CALIFORNIA

The ULTIMATE VICTORIANS of the Continental Side
of San Francisco Bay

Printed and bound in the United States of America

Library of Congress Catalog Card No. 71-139213

ISBN 0-8310-7081-1

Second Printing, December, 1970

Published by Howell-North Books
1050 Parker Street, Berkeley, California 94710

FOR

CLYDE AMMONS RICHEY

Acknowledgments

The author wishes to thank the following institutions and individuals for their assistance.

ALAMEDA COUNTY HISTORICAL SOCIETY
ALAMEDA FREE LIBRARY
ALAMEDA HISTORICAL SOCIETY
THE ALAMEDA TIMES STAR
BANCROFT LIBRARY
BERKELEY ART COMMISSION
BERKELEY CHAMBER OF COMMERCE
THE BERKELEY DAILY GAZETTE
BERKELEY PUBLIC LIBRARY
JUNIOR LEAGUE OF OAKLAND
OAKLAND CITY MANAGER'S OFFICE
OAKLAND MUSEUM
OAKLAND PUBLIC LIBRARY
THE OAKLAND TRIBUNE
THE SOCIETY OF CALIFORNIA PIONEERS
MRS. JULIA COOLEY ALTROCCHI
MRS. FRANCES BUXTON
MR. KENNETH CARDWELL
DR. ELLIOT EVANS
MISS EVELYN GOLDSTEIN
MR. A. LEWIS KOUE
MRS. AUGUSTIN C. KEANE
MR. PAUL A. LIEBHART
MRS. A. HUBBARD MOFFITT, JR.
MRS. ALBERT NORMAN
MRS. JACQUES MARX
MRS. HENRIETTA PERRY
MRS. WILLIAM QUINN
MR. LOUIS STEIN
MR. LEONARD VERBARG
MRS. JANE VOILES

Contents

Introduction

There was a time, earlier in this century, when it was fashionable to grimace at any mention of the Victorian Era, that period that began in the halcyon interval before the Civil War and rounded the turn-of-the-century. It was supposed to have reached a cultural nadir and to have produced a setting of unspeakable hideousness. This condescending attitude toward the era he had depicted so vividly in many of his novels and plays, once roused Sir James Barrie to this sage rejoinder: "Don't forget to speak scornfully of the Victorian Age; there will be time for meekness when you try to better it."

Now, of course, the need for defense or apology no longer exists. Successively, the Victorian Age has passed through the stages of the vilified, the fascinatingly curious, and into the realm of the popular. Whether we consciously concede that we indeed have failed to better it, we are in large and increasing numbers looking back with affection and admiration upon that bygone time.

The aim of this book is to recapture that intriguing era and to offer the reader an opportunity to explore it in the company of a writer who frankly admires the time and shows a penetrating understanding of it. This book is neither a complete reference work nor a pavane for a vanished society, but rather a most entertaining examination of selected facets of the architectural, social and art history of that age to which we are all closely related. Today, it is apparent that the origins of most of our accomplishments in this century had their roots in those rich and vital years.

It is appropriate that Elinor Richey, who has written widely on nineteenth century architecture and on city environment, chose to recreate the era by focusing especially on the homes the Victorians built and lived in. For she believes we reveal our character through our cultural preferences and that it is a region's architecture that most accurately reflects its history and the quality of its inhabitants.

Of no less significance is her choice of setting. She has focused on a place that, in her opinion, reached an apogee of Victorian expression, both in its domestic architecture and in its culture. Her setting is the area that lies on the Continental side of San Francisco Bay and is popularly called "East Bay." The East Bay is made up of terrains of quite different character — the sandy flatland and the stony hills of the Coast Range. Both the "flats" and the westward slopes are now almost totally blanketed with cities that had their beginnings as settlements roughly in the mid-nineteenth century.

The settlers were drawn to an El Dorado of natural blessings — balmy climate, incredibly fertile soil, breath-takingly beautiful hills that alternated during the two seasons, rainy and rainless, from tawny brown knolls to green pastures with blue and purple lupine, and, of course, at its rim the lovely, tranquil Bay. Before the century ended, the settlements had attained such phenomenal development that they were almost contiguous with one another. Further, the East Bay had nurtured in its midst one of the country's greatest universities, the University of California.

The prolonged building boom that created the East Bay coincided almost exactly with the revolution in the construction industry — the rapid introduction of new tools, new materials, new processes. It further coincided with the swiftest and most dazzling succession of residential architecture styles that the world has ever seen. These forces from without combined with the unique influences of the district — with its abundant wealth, its cultural aspirations, and its permissive climate — to produce the arresting buildings that we have called The Ultimate Victorians.

We are fortunate that a great many of these dwellings still exist in our East Bay cities. As a Boston Back Bay matron once said, "We do not *buy* our hats — we *have* them," so do we have and treasure, like the heirlooms that they are, our Victorian houses. We treasure them the more for knowing their likes will not be built again, both because of economic factors and a decline of hand-craftsmanship in the building arts.

Perhaps too in the matter of their regaining our affection is a new appreciation of Victorian manners and mores in contrast to our free-wheeling, uncertain society of today. The Victorians were fiercely individualistic, vigorous, and far-sighted, yet they had an aura of grace. It is in nostalgic remembrance of them and their times that this book is offered.

The Publishers

Bret Harte once lived and wrote his colorful Gold Rush tales across the street from these houses on the 500 block on Fifth Street in Oakland, not far from present Jack London Square. When they were restored by an investment group, organized by Mrs. Paul Mills (who penned this delightful sketch), the block was named for the popular author. Today these handsome Victorian houses, all built between 1860 and 1880, are honeycombed with distinctive shops, galleries, tearooms and restaurants.

The luxuriant East Bay rambling rose could encircle a cottage or a giant arbor. To stroll down this inviting rose arbor walk was one of the pleasures of Oakland's popular May Day Fetes. For years, they were a spring event on the grounds of Arbor Villa, the vast Oakland estate of the world-famous "Borax King" F. M. Smith. *(Jane Voiles collection)*

Peacocks and Porticos

We've no idea what age we are living in, nor what we shall one day be called. Just as Giotto never guessed as he brushed foreground figures in a Padua atelier that he was ushering in the Renaissance. Even an aproned guildsman on a cathedral scaffold fitting a pointed stone had no inkling he was sitting in the middle of the Middle Ages. All we know for certain is that the "Modern Age" is only a temporary name tag. Every age confidently calls itself modern. Whatever our age may be, it will just have to await a christening by some future historian.

However, history does illustrate that a sign one age is creaking to an end is its rediscovery of the age that it repudiated; by then the cycle is nearing completion. We have been exuberantly, energetically, and expectantly rediscovering the Victorian Age. Especially we have been rediscovering the art, decoration, and architecture of the latter half of the nineteenth century, whose name historians purloined from the very proper British queen and gave to that age of pomp and sentiment.

Every imaginable Victorian object, from hatpins to gazebos, is being zealously collected. Portieres and carnival glass, even dingy daguerrotypes, have been promoted from the attic back into the parlor, after a shockingly expensive detour to the antique shop. Antique dealers are hanging out-of-sight prices on Tiffany lamps, once seen mainly as props on movie sets of Gay Nine-

ties bordellos. Department stores promote less expensive Tiffany reproductions, along with painstakingly exact replicas of heavy Victorian sofas and sideboards. New York's glittering culturati crowds into velvet-draped auction rooms on Fifty-seventh Street on Saturday afternoons to bid jealously on nineteenth century paintings that a few years back were catching dust in storage rooms. And, of course, the advertising industry has almost lasciviously embraced the voluptuous curves of Art Nouveau.

Similarly with architecture. Victorian mansions, once scorned and forgotten, are being lovingly restored with patient lifting of hastily-splashed paint and tireless sleuthing for missing dados and bargeboards and balustrade rungs. Likely as not, that patient restorer is a shrewd real estate operator who has found that filigreed facades rent for thrice the rate of stripped-down models. In cities across the country, restored Victorian houses and apartments are being vied for by the smart set. Among boastful occupants are fashionable architects who hide behind the gingerbread by night from the geometry they must perpetrate by day.

However, there is one crucial difference in the current state of Victorian houses and Victorian artifacts. Preserving a house is infinitely more difficult than preserving a lamp. No contractor has stepped forward to reproduce a Victorian house, nor is likely to; economics precludes it. For all

11

During their first years of settlement, the Yankees didn't improve the scenery. Here is Oakland's Broadway in the 1860s. One summer visitor went away complaining Oakland possessed "a great natural wealth of sand and fleas." But in winter the complaint was of mud, in which horses mired and pigs wallowed. *(Albert Norman collection)*

Precursor of California's singing eucalyptus groves was this tree which grew from a seed planted in Alameda in 1863. While on missionary travels for the Methodist church, Bishop William Taylor sent home a packet of seeds from Australia. His wife presented them to family friends, among them Dr. W. P. Gibbons, who coaxed his seedling into this bunchy 125-foot specimen. *(Alameda Historical Society)*

their cultural cachet, Victorian houses are dwindling daily.

The reasons are several. Neglect of a house may have advanced too far to be reversed with paint and lumber. And what with present population pressures, older residential districts are being rezoned to permit apartment buildings; when this happens property taxes soar and developers' offers grow tempting. Also forever bearing down on older districts is some public building project — an institution, street, or highway — that irresistibly shunts aside all in its way. The Victorian houses in our midst are in jeopardy; some say their days are numbered. Fearing we have learned to love them again only to lose them, we rush to savor their charms before they disappear forever.

What is their special essence, these houses toward which the pendulum of taste has returned? Whose very name "Victorian" summons a dramatic silhouette in every mind's eye, and conjures up an aura so vivid it is almost tangible. What creates this special excitement?

For one thing, they are boldly individualistic — like the Victorians themselves, who were unconcerned with subtlety. They have an almost commanding presence. Build a sleek modern house beside one of these proud mansions, and the Victorian will dominate the scene like a seasoned character actress who steals the show from the bland leading lady.

The charge that Victorian houses were conforming carbon copies is grossly uninformed. Never before spilled such a cornucopia of variety. Victorian wasn't one style but many, a restless ever-waxing-and-waning procession of residential styles borrowed from every corner of the world, from every era of history. Victorian residential styles came and went like ladies' hats, and each style was an escapist dream, a flight into the idyllic long ago, or to the strange and distant. One dream dissolved into the next.

How could anyone have called them somber? In their debutante days they were vividly and fancifully colorful; indeed, some were veritable rainbows. Nor is the charge of pretentiousness really valid, when these houses so gayly and forthrightly pretended — to be villas, to be chateaux, to be fortified castles, or thatched Elizabethan cottages. Of course, they pretended. That was part of their fun.

California Victorians had an extra measure of fun and audacity. Indeed, the rich architectural brew called Victorian transcended itself in the Golden State; architectural scholars agree that Victorian domestic architecture reached its most luxuriant flowering in California. As New Zealanders with their high teas are said to be more English than the English, California builders more successfully than did English and East Coast builders released the full spirit of the Victorian house.

It was an optimistic era, but nowhere did optimism ride higher than in the cocky new state, vibrating with gold strikes, silver bonanzas, wheat coups, railroad triumphs, and rumors of even greater things to come. Regretfully, the loot wasn't universally abundant, but, oh, the spirit was, and the same don't-do-it-halfway boldness that wrote the bonanza legends contributed to some truly astonishing residential architecture. The man who had batched in a blanket lean-to in Hangtown frankly aspired to something extraordinary. Returned to the Bay Area with his poke full of gold dust, he was still too busy expanding his fortune to make the Continental Grand Tour, but he could shop from the tempting boutique of imported styles and choose one to suit his fancy. Architects zestfully obliged him. Speak the word and he might have his own private tower, or ramparts to pace upon.

San Francisco, being the pulsing center of the California spectacular, would have been the natural setting for this voluptuous Victorian flowering, but for a stern real estate fact. San Francisco was virtually born into a land squeeze — all those tens of thousands of gold-bedazzled adventurers and speculators swarming up from ships in the harbor, all jockeying for vantage points, the better to hear the latest gold strike rumor. This tussle for space, rather like in Roman-occupied Bethlehem at taxpaying time, early clamped a pattern of narrow lot development over the sand hills. And lots of twenty to twenty-five feet wide just weren't conducive to real Victorian houses, which demanded ungirdling room — room to spill out with verandas, side wings, porticos, conservatories, solariums, and porte-cochères. Narrow lots even crimped the

Victorian predilection for towers, which looked foolish soaring up from skimpy underpinnings. San Francisco simply lacked the physical space to release the spirit of a true Victorian.

What San Francisco's slim lots were conducive to, of course, was row housing, that practical design by which dwellings were built each-to-each, and San Francisco architects did something truly creative with that New England staple. By fashioning house fronts and rears narrower than their aligning middles, they permitted sun-inviting side windows. Interior light, so valued on the fog-swept hills, was further coaxed with the bay window, which San Francisco architects surely carried to its highest potential, even if they didn't actually invent it, as is sometimes claimed. These elaborate projections swelled downward and outward until the city was obliged to pass an ordinance limiting their extension toward the street. A visiting English correspondent once described the "stately fronts . . . with all the windows gracefully leaping out of themselves." Architects dressed these row house facades with a tasteful mixture of French, Italian, and Corinthian details, attaining an elegant composition that became known as the San Francisco style. A delightful concoction, but it wasn't true Victorian.

Where California Victorian really blossomed, raised its stamens, unfurled its tendrils, spread its lushest petals was in the San Francisco suburbs. And most of all in the East Bay suburbs of Oakland, Alameda, and Berkeley. These leafy communities on the rolling slopes of the Coast Range gained a far-flung reputation for their "elegant mansions and tasteful cottages." The broad, shady avenues offered one of the not-to-be-missed sights for visitors to the West, who ferried over and hired carriages from which to view the genteel domiciles and marvel at the contrast with the wild interior towns they had traveled through. Magazines sent their roving reporters to sketch and photograph the prepossessing facades and to describe the grand salons, ballrooms, and art galleries for readers avid for a glimpse into the lives of the California *nouveaux riches*. Decorative etchings of the fine houses were featured in those fancy albums of engravings that were so popular with Victorians for leisurely parlor perusal.

The burgeoning suburban community contrasted even more with its historically recent past. The Spanish had called the eastern side of San Francisco Bay the *contra costa* (opposite shore). During the halcyon days of the Spanish missions, the padres pastured their cattle on its hills and grassy flats to support their monastic communities in San Jose and San Francisco. By the time of the Gold Rush, it was enveloped by sprawling Rancho San Antonio, domain of the storied Peraltas, father and sons and their multitudinous families. Don Peralta had acquired his 45,000 acres in 1820 in a grant from the Spanish Crown, a reward for long and faithful military service at the San Francisco Presidio.

Depending on which historian you read, the Peralta casas were sumptuous abodes of costly hangings and elegant carven furniture, the setting of grand balls and gay fiestas with ruffle-twirling senoritas dancing and castaneting, and svelte caballeros arching like fiddle bows from horses to swoop gold pieces from the ground. Or they were crude, dirt-floored adobes whose sluggish occupants eked a meager living bartering tallow and hides when a ship happened to anchor in the Bay.

One thing is certain, however. The Peraltas wanted no part of the gold rush, neither its glittering ore (if God had wanted *them* to have it, Don Peralta sternly adjured his sons, he'd have *shown* it to them), nor the Yankee invaders (money-mad non-believers). While they were spared the former, there was no escaping the latter. Disappointed prospectors wandering back from the Sierra diggings not only squatted wherever they pleased on Peralta land, but, adding insult to injury, turned their ill humor derisively upon the helpless don as he galloped frantically about on his fine horse with its silver-mounted saddle and fancy trappings imperiously pointing the way off his ranch. History was against him. Pio Pico, the last Mexican governor of California, had already surrendered to General Frémont, and late in 1850 Congress would vote to admit California to the Union.

Rancho San Antonio went the way of the missions, into legend. The beleaguered Peraltas, by one means or another, were contained in small dwelling plots, where, finally reconciled, they tried to emulate the gringos. They abandoned

"When the Yankees came in and the courteous Spaniard greeted him at the door with '*La casa es suya*' (The house is yours), the Yankee took him literally and seized everything in sight. . . . Thus it was with things in all directions, the Spanish scarcely uttering a protest, until at last the great ranches themselves were swallowed up."— *Julia Cooley Altrocchi*

No match for the aggressive gringo was frail, five-foot-tall Ignacio Peralta, the eldest of the Peralta sons. Although his part of the divided Rancho San Antonio stretched over East Oakland and part of San Leandro, he soon found himself confined to a small plot on San Leandro Creek. But after his daughter married an American, she built him this snug house, the first brick building in the county, in a combined Spanish and American style. The brick sides and shingle roof, then considered more stylish than the American-scorned adobe and tile, have since been replaced by adobe-like stucco and American-made tile. Located at Leo and Lafayette Streets in San Leandro, it now houses the Alta Mira Club and is a State Historical Landmark, open weekdays to visitors by appointment. (*National Parks Service*)

15

Here are the west parlor, the molded ceiling medallion and vestibule of the house where Ignacio Peralta spent his old age. There was little in this proper Victorian setting to remind him of his youth as a golden-spurred ranchero. *(National Parks Service)*

Whaleboats rowed by hand were the first ferries to connect the East Bay with San Francisco. But steamboat ferries soon followed, at first making one return trip a day. After rival ferries began operating, one pilot would try to run his competition onto the sand bar at the mouth of the Oakland Estuary, and some pilots kept rifles handy to ensure "cooperation." One early ferryboat was "The Oakland," which had served as the river steamer "Chrysopolis" until it was purchased by the Central Pacific Railroad in the 1870s and rebuilt into a double end ferry. Rebuilt again in 1920 to accommodate autos, "The Oakland" served longer than any other ferry on the Bay. *(Oakland Public Library)*

their tile-roofed adobes, so scorned by the new-comers. In San Leandro, Ignacio Péralta built a red brick house with a shingle roof; in Oakland, both Vincent and Antonio Peralta built frame houses, both painted bright yellow; while in Berkeley, Domingo Peralta camouflaged his adobe with a cast-iron front imported from the Eastern Seaboard.

The East Bay became blanketed with truck farms and orchards to supply the San Francisco market. For San Franciscans the Contra Costa was also an idyllic place to row or sail to on a Sunday to escape the fog and wind. The visitors picnicked under the trees, so missed in barren San Francisco, and gathered wild flowers to carry home. Their visits grew longer and more frequent. Soon week-end and vacation cottages were tucked here and there among the luxuriant oak groves. Hotels and restaurants began catering to the holi-day crowd.

In time, the leisured and affluent began to build grand country estates secluded in the hills and canyons. When ferries began churning the Bay on regular schedules, even those tied to San Francisco businesses and professions could make their homes in the East Bay and commute to the city. The Spanish rancho quickly evolved into a genteel American suburb.

Those who early chose to make a permanent crossing to the eastern shore were from the cream of San Francisco's social and business communi-ties, polished men with interests stretching to Alaska, to South America, to Australia, to the Orient. These men of means and influence shared another common denominator. Perhaps because of its special appeals as a place of natural beauty and solitude, the district exerted a particular magnetism for bookish types — for aesthetes, scholars, patrons of the arts; for nature lovers who netted butterflies, bird-watched, collected mineral specimens; for amateur astronomers and fresh-air enthusiasts; and, yes, for the recluse and the eccentric.

These cultivated, individualistic personalities reflected not only in the houses they built for themselves, but equally in the lavish gardens with which they surrounded their grand abodes. For whatever their other cultural bents, these new-comers either brought, or promptly acquired, an enthusiasm for horticulture. The encouraging soil no doubt had been one of the community's en-ticements; San Francisco's small lots and sandy soil frustrated the botanical pursuits that were so popular with Victorians.

Gardening for pleasure had originated early in the nineteenth century in England, as a con-

Oakland's first store was a small tent covered with hides, its first city hall a rented room, while the Sunday church services were conducted under an oak tree. This house proudly preserved as Oakland's first frame residence actually was constructed around the first, a rude cottage thrown up in 1849 by Moses Chase, who came over from San Francisco to hunt and fish. *(Oakland Public Library)*

The peaceful country lane below that winds through a dense thicket of pin oaks was at the site of Berkeley's present Shattuck Avenue where it crosses Cordonices Creek. *(Louis Stein collection)*

Going, going . . . to make way for modern Kaiser Center is the old College of the Holy Names. In its proud stance above, it had been a familiar Oakland landmark on the northeast rim of Lake Merritt since its erection in 1872 by the Sisters of the Holy Names of Jesus and Mary, who came to Oakland in 1868 to start their school. Sadly, economics is knocking on many another venerable door. Thus the noble and dignified old Victorian buildings that lend dignity and variety to the urban panorama and give a sense of continuity and permanence to our lives are rapidly diminishing. *(California Historical Society)*

By the 1870s, Oakland's business district was centered on Ninth Street between Washington and Broadway in this block (north side above), which constituted a veritable museum of commercial architecture styles of the Mid-Victorian era. The street's wide range of businesses included an ice cream parlor, wine and liquor shop, cigar stand, Wells Fargo branch, photographer, attorney, and lodging houses. Pioneer developer Frederick Delger erected the building on the right corner, which in 1870 housed the Oakland *News*, the city's first newspaper. (*From Illustrated Directory of Oakland, California*)

trived diversion for males to keep them out of the tavern, but by mid-century it had become fashionable for both men and women to dabble in horticulture. Ladies' periodicals had persuaded genteel women that such an interest was not beneath them. Indeed, it was uplifting. Plants and flowers were said to educate via "intelligent observation of the floral parts," and to "teach the lesson of patient submission, meek endurance, and innocent cheerfulness under the pressure of adverse circumstances." Such appeals impressed Victorians, who liked to be ethically motivated.

A conservatory was part of the typical East Bay Victorian home, whether an attached glass wing or a great domed and compartmented greenhouse. Every owner had his prize specialties — orchids, gardenias, tropical plants, rare fern. One connoisseur specialized in rare California specimens. Topping the grand array, on the conservatory ceiling climbed the violet-blossomed passion flower vine, much favored by Victorians for its religious connotation (its stamen vaguely defined a cross).

Oakland quickly gained a reputation for having the finest and best-stocked conservatories in California, and locally the competition was heated for top horticultural honors. A. K. P. Harmon, the Maine-born financier and philanthropist who endowed Harmon Gymnasium at the University of California, opened his grand conservatory that flanked his Lake Merritt mansion for the edification of Oakland school children. Frederick Delger,

Oakland's first multi-millionaire, could offer guests at his fabulous Telegraph Avenue estate the visual treat presented by his collection of camellias and azaleas, after which they might divert themselves in his commodious aviary twittering with birds of rare and brilliant plumage.

But sprawling outdoor flower gardens, everywhere flaming blossoms and exuding fragrance, were the East Bay's crowning glory. In late afternoon, merchants and lawyers, comfortable in shirt sleeves, contentedly wielded trowels and pruning shears. Women liked to promenade amongst their flowers with their friends, all prettily twirling parasols. Mornings found them bent over blossoms with basket and scissors, snipping a bouquet for the dining table or to fashion into one of the tightly-packed spheres, cones, or mushroom-shaped knobs of flowers that were part of every evening costume.

Garden favorites were the big, showy flowers: dahlias, heliotrope, hydrangeas, broad-leaved cannas, zinnias, hollyhocks, large cacti. Victorians tended to prefer blossoms that were plump and round, qualities much admired in feminine contours. Almost forgotten today but much fancied then were the bulky, beruffled coxcomb and the overblown calceolaria, whose golden blossoms resembled little speckled balloons. The East Bay also doted on geraniums, favoring those with varicolored leaves; when set in a bed the riot of leaves and flowers resembled a gaudy Afghan shawl. The Oakland *Enquirer* reported that one

The entrance to the Frederick Delger mansion on Telegraph Avenue is landscaped in the formal Italian style preferred by East Bay home owners during the early Victorian era. In a special issue directed at Eastern investors, the Oakland *Enquirer* boasted of the grand Delger estate with its lawns "as beautiful as a green velvet carpet." *(Jane Voiles collection)*

Below is the private conservatory of A. K. P. Harmon, who took prizes for his horticultural specimens. Harmon later gave it to the City of Oakland, and it became an attraction in Lakeside Park at a site now occupied by the Veterans Memorial. *(Albert Norman collection)*

This century-old house in the French Mansard style at 911 Grand Avenue in Alameda was in a state of shabby dilapidation when it was purchased by the A. Hubbard Moffitts and lovingly restored. The carriage house was made into a triple garage. Mrs. Moffitt became so enamoured with the French architectural scheme that she furnished the house throughout with Louis XVI furniture, including a commode that is a replica of one owned by Marie Antoinette. (*Mrs. A. Hubbard Moffitt, Jr.*)

A strong persuader for the purchase and restoration was the fine finishing of the house's interior, which attests to the high skill of nineteenth century craftsmen. Three of the rooms have beautifully sculpted white marble fireplaces. The parquet floors are of golden oak in an intricate interlacing pattern. The hardware (note door and keyhole) is of molded gold-bronze. One of the door panels of etched glass, shown below, was broken. But diligent search located a retired Oakland glass cutter who duplicated the panel exactly. *(Mrs. A. Hubbard Moffitt, Jr.)*

The peaceful grounds of the Oakland estate of Banker Henry Douglas Bacon at Tenth and Oak streets spread over nearly four acres. Bacon endowed the University of California's early Bacon Hall, which housed the library and art gallery. The estate's first owner was Benjamin Horn, uncle of Gertrude Atherton, who described it in her book ADVENTURES OF A NOVELIST. *(Jane Voiles collection)*

aficionado of that fuzzy, acrid plant cultivated no less than twenty-four thriving varieties. Power not lyricism was the gardener's goal, and there was no hesitation in mixing the strongest colors. Red, pink, and purple blossoms bobbed side by side, and a bower of sky-blue hydrangea was likely to be encircled with a border of scarlet geranium.

It was the height of gardening chic to import rare exotics, especially shrubs and trees, and a surprising number of plants from such places as New Zealand, Africa, South America, and the Indies took to the soil like natives. Thanks to this vogue, today more than half of the garden foliage in the East Bay is foreign. Newcomers from the East found their taste for the exotic quite appeased with the miraculous effects of the virgin soil on ordinary flowers. They found East Bay gardening a never-ending revelation, what with its surprise-box of man-high calla lilies, basketball-sized dahlias, and lemon verbena that shot up tree-tall.

However, selecting one's flowers was simpler than choosing a landscaping style, that is deciding which of three sanctioned garden arrangements to apply. It was no small decision, and almost irreversible. The most frequent choice in the suburb's early days was the Italian formal garden, a geometric arrangement of squared-off gravel terraces and grass plots, these intersected with arrow-straight bordered walks. Precisely spaced here and there were classical flowering urns, sculpture, and fountains with accompanying stone seats from which to contemplate them. This garden with the air of an outdoor drawing room was developed under the Romans, revived during the Renaissance, then again in seventeenth-century France in the garden of Versailles. The Italian garden appealed to Victorian formality.

Or the choice might be an English "natural" garden, a landscape scheme which feigned the effect of natural growth with irregular settings of flowers, fern, and shrubs in uneven clumps, this cut through by mossy paths, winding and crossing as though beat by woodland creatures. This style, which developed in eighteenth-century England, appealed to the more romantic taste. The Berkeley writer Charles Keeler argued that the natural garden exuded "a purer sentiment, a more refined love of nature undefiled, than can be obtained by more artificial means." Some Victorians, while keeping their own passions fettered, preferred nature wild and unfettered, and paid dearly to have a landscaper plan and replan until their garden concealed all plan and resembled some bosky dell one chanced upon while netting butterflies. A triumph of studied casualness! Amidst the disciplined disorder young lovers wandered hand in hand vibrantly quoting Wordsworth.

24

This was the fern and orchid corner of F. M. Smith's private conservatory. Cultivating hot house plants was an approved hobby for Victorian gentlemen, but women liked it too, for it permitted them to love nature, along with Emerson and Thoreau, without exposing their delicate complexions to the out-of-doors. Thus conservatories were a must for those who could afford them. Those who couldn't sometimes created the illusion of one by bedecking the parlor with tall house plants and by cultivating ivy in planters and coaxing it to grow on arbors arched over a sofa or love seat. *(Oakland Public Library)*

These gardens afforded a wide choice of trysting places: latticed archways, weeping willows, rustic gazebos, vine-covered arbors, arbors of hanging baskets trailing feathery fern. The natural garden overtook the Italian garden during the high Victorian era and has lingered with us, although in a modified, practical form. American landscape artists today generally work in the spirit of the English natural garden.

East Bay Victorians of a more authoritarian mold sometimes preferred to cultivate a German garden. This ordered landscaping scheme was also known as carpet-bedding, because its chief feature was beds in which plants and flowers were trimmed and disciplined until they looked as smooth as carpets. Plant materials were selected and combined for their uniform habits of low growth and for their vivid colors.

25

For those who tired of their conventional Italian or English garden, there were landscaping alternatives. One was an "Arizona garden" with desert plants, such as this one, at right, on the grounds of the Frank C. Havens' home in Piedmont. Another landscaping scheme popular in the East Bay in the late Victorian era was the Japanese garden. It was a miniature copy of nature with its mimic mountains and lakes, its bonsai trees and stones, and artificial watercourse spanned by arching bridges. (*Albert Norman collection*)

The Victorians doted on water lilies and many an estate had its lily pond. This one ornamented the grounds at Arbor Villa. The exotic blossom also figured prominently indoors in carpet and upholstery design. The craze was sparked by that botanical wonder, the "Victoria Regia," the world's largest water lily that was named after Queen Victoria. One of the giant lilies was brought from its native British Guiana to bloom in Golden Gate Park and everybody went to marvel at its out-sized rose-white blossoms and its giant leaves that would support a child. (*Jane Voiles collection*)

These beds, set amidst immaculate green lawns, were given the geometric shapes of circles, stars, triangles, or crescents. Within these rigid forms flowers of contrasting colors were employed, like tapestry wools, to define more intricate designs such as butterflies, birds, even flower forms. Outlining these gardens was a "ribbon border," a narrow floral strip in variegated colors.

For some, these contrived formalities constituted the ultimate in gardening elegance. But after several decades of mild popularity, they became déclassé for residential landscaping. One still finds an occasional carpet garden, in a small railroad park, or in a formal public garden such as that in San Francisco's Civic Center and the one on the grounds of the Chancellor's mansion at the University of California at Berkeley, which features a gay floral clock. Industrial firms sometimes employ them for advertising, cultivating a brilliant floral trademark before a company headquarters.

Whatever the landscaping scheme and architectural style finally settled upon by the discriminating newcomer, the effect was thought to be magnificently enhanced by a peacock in the foreground, strutting and preening and spreading its jewel-toned tail, confidently the cynosure, even amidst the feast of carpet-bedding, geranium borders, and playing fountains. During the Victorian Era the peacock served durably as an East Bay status symbol.

Yet for all its cultivated tone and lush beauty, the East Bay probably would long have remained a pastoral, sparsely-populated family suburb, and a rather isolated one, but for a marvelous stroke of luck. It came from without, lifting the district overnight from the rank of mere bedroom for San Francisco to that of a place that held a commanding importance in its own right. Further, this new acquisition presented the East Bay the potential to even rival its haughty neighbor. This arrival was, of course, the world-watched transcontinental railroad, the "Big Four's" hard-won Central Pacific. The miraculous shining span linked the East Bay directly with rich and sophisticated New York City and made San Francisco sit up and take an envious new look at its quiet *contra costa*.

'The house of doom' some called John Marsh's Gothic mansion near Mount Diablo. It seemed to harbor tragedy for the family that built it. After arriving in the 1840s when the Mexicans still ruled California, he wrote home to New England: "I possess at this place a farm about ten miles by twelve miles in extent. I have at last found the Far West and intend to end my ramblings here." Several years later he found a bride, and it was for her that he built the great stone house, but she never occupied it. (*Oakland* TRIBUNE)

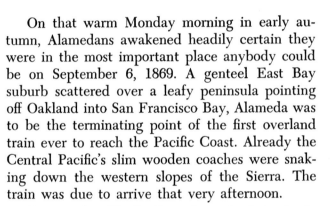

From Tents to Towers

On that warm Monday morning in early autumn, Alamedans awakened headily certain they were in the most important place anybody could be on September 6, 1869. A genteel East Bay suburb scattered over a leafy peninsula pointing off Oakland into San Francisco Bay, Alameda was to be the terminating point of the first overland train ever to reach the Pacific Coast. Already the Central Pacific's slim wooden coaches were snaking down the western slopes of the Sierra. The train was due to arrive that very afternoon.

By a stroke of luck, Alameda at the last minute had won the terminal away from Oakland, after Oakland had won it away from San Francisco. First plans had called for connecting the transcontinental railroad with a local in San Jose; later, plans for a terminal on Goat Island fell through. The switch to Alameda had come so abruptly there scarcely had been time to prepare a proper welcome. But then changes and delays had been the rule on the Central Pacific's last lap, the 100-mile stretch from Sacramento to the Bay. Unlinked track had sprawled amidst valley wild flowers long after construction gangs had conquered the inland mountains and Indians and buffalo herds. That gold spike they had driven in Utah four months before had not really connected the Atlantic and the Pacific, as the press agents had so dramatically claimed. Train passengers found themselves obliged to alight at Sacramento

and board a river boat, which chugged downstream for eight hours before reaching the Coast.

For the final stretch of that last lap, the Central Pacific had bought out an East Bay local, the San Francisco & Alameda Rail Road that ran from Hayward to the Alameda wharf, with the idea of constructing an extension from the local to a terminating point at the Oakland ferry wharf. But then *that* project delayed in starting, and after starting hit a snag. Thus the surprise decision to run the train into Alameda.

As they scanned the skies above the drying oaks and poplars, Alamedans agreed the day would be fine, unlike that May afternoon the rails were joined in Utah. First, pounding rains had nearly washed away the tracks; then came howling, frigid winds which kept celebrants scurrying to warm themselves at stove and bottle and so shivered Governor Stanford that his hammer missed the gold spike and the omission had to be covered with a sound effect. California weather could be counted on, even if it wasn't, as foolishly reported in the East, a magic essence in which beets swelled the size of human heads and native-born males grew to seven feet. When the train rolled in, the sun would be shining brightly in the western sky.

Something else would shine on Alameda and the whole East Bay — the spotlight of fame. It was hoped fervently that the switch to Alameda would be permanent. Alamedans considered it appropriate that they should be juxtaposed to fashionable New York City. They pridefully recalled that the $14,000 two Yankee settlers had paid the Spanish for Alameda was handsomer remuneration than the twenty-four dollars the Indians got for Manhattan. Of course, Oakland, Alameda's adjoining neighbor, would share the glory, as well as budding Berkeley, where preparations were underway for a new campus for the University of California, now cramped in downtown Oakland.

The eastern shore was touchily conscious of being considered a mere appendage of San Francisco, whose ties to the world being via ship insisted on thinking of the opposite mainland as a sort of island. So did water-arriving visitors to California. The recent dispatch of a roving Eastern journalist had characterized Oakland as "the Staten Island of the Bay Region." Island, indeed! The continent-girdling railroad would set geography aright.

It would set the East Bay's image aright too. The attention the terminal would draw would spotlight the East Bay's splendid assets, which had never been accorded their proper due. Except, of course, by its own proud denizens who congratulated themselves upon having created the most idyllic life style in California, their enjoyment marred only by San Francisco's patronizing attitude.

How could San Francisco fail to notice just how *au courant* the East Bay was in residential fashion? Its houses were constructed in the very same modes then in favor on the advanced Eastern Seaboard, where high-columned Greek Revival had been edged out by two other revival styles. The vogue now was for high, spikey Gothic houses and for wide, towered Italian villas, both irregular, rambling styles which required plenty of room. Fortunately land was both cheap and abundant in the East Bay. A tourist guidebook published in New York described Oakland houses of the period as "standing detached and usually surrounded by a liberal expanse of gardens, grass-plat and shrubbery which reminds one of an Eastern village."

Thus the history-making train would be arriving in a society that grandly gazed out at the world from houses inspired by medieval castles and cathedrals and from villas such as had housed the merchant princes of Renaissance Florence. If San Francisco would only look, it couldn't fail to be impressed. Quite obviously it *hadn't*, for it continued to confuse the East Bay with the character of its unfortunate early beginnings.

Admittedly, things couldn't have gotten off to a worse start. First, there had been that grubby business of the squatters and the jumpers. Defeated prospectors drifting back from the mines had squatted on Peralta lands along the waterfront, scrappily defying Spanish efforts to oust them. The squatters, in turn, were plagued by men seeking to jump their stolen toe holds. Their ceaseless brawling in the mud flats was the laughing stock of San Francisco. Finally, the squatters organized for mutual protection, going so far as to acquire a cannon. Whereupon, the jumpers organized, and one night, making a surprise attack, they managed to seize the weapon. East Bay history today might read with quite a different cast had not the jumpers omitted to purloin some ammunition, an oversight which foiled their grab and inspired the daughter of one of the squatters to pen a commemorative poem: "They stole our only cannon and brought it from the hall. But when they went to fire it, they had forgot the ball."

By the time all the squatting and jumping and unauthorized selling subsided, land titles were in a woeful tangle. A buyer might be obliged to pay off a half-dozen claimants before he felt secure enough to build, and even then might lose all when some late pettifoger managed to establish a claim. Thus respectable professional men often found themselves in the undignified position of being accused of squatting. A widow who had invested her nest egg in a modest cottage at Fourteenth and Broadway, now Oakland's chief intersection, was awakened in the dead of night by loud rappings of a belated claimant with sheriff's eviction crew. Hiding in the attic and copiously sobbing and pleading didn't save her from being tossed into the street like some drunken interloper, along with all she owned.

But unquestionably the most troublesome of the East Bay's misfortunes was a long-persisting one in the person of one Horace Carpentier, a New York lawyer who practiced briefly in San

Gothic gables dominate the panorama in this 1869 photograph of Oakland, looking northeast from the College of California campus. Lake Merritt may be glimpsed in the right background beneath the barren Oakland hills. Oakland already boasted one paved street (a macadamized strip on Broadway from the wharf up to Fourteenth Street), it had installed its first sewer, had a library association making plans for a library, and that year would get its first city directory. But it still didn't own a city hall. *(Albert Norman collection)*

Francisco before descending upon unsuspecting Oakland. With his slender figure, blue eyes, prim mouth, and thin aristocratic nose, Carpentier looked the consummate gentleman, which aspect together with his pose of willing helper gained him entry wherever he wished. Having gained entry he proceeded quietly to confiscate whatever it was he wanted. In probing the slippery Carpentier character, the researcher is rather reminded of the Roman politician Catiline, who was described as "polished in manners, beautiful in person, of pleasing intellect, and a mind ever intent on evil."

Although he himself was a squatter upon Don Peralta's land, Carpentier, who spoke fluent Spanish, represented himself as a former priest and persuaded the bewildered patriarch to let him offer protection from the other squatters. Evenings he visited the Peralta casa and, kneeling, surrounded by the reverently admiring family, would unctuously recite the rosary. Between prayers, the humble don placidly signed away a sizable portion of his rancho in the belief he was signing a power of attorney which would enable the good father to protect his interests.

Likewise, partly by charm, partly by chicanery, Carpentier persuaded early Oaklanders, who were valiantly trying to unmuddle the town's affairs, that he would dedicate his law skills to Oakland's welfare, if only they would turn things over to him. Even Carpentier must have been amazed at their trustfulness. In succession, they assigned to him their entire water front, the exclusive franchise to provide ferry service, and the

31

right to operate a toll bridge across the slough behind the town. The eager helper thus invested himself with powers not unlike those medieval feudal lords who extorted tribute from all who traversed their borders. By this time Oakland was on to "Nefarious Horace," and angry citizens took to clotting together in assault groups and storming his toll gates. But their pains won them only howls of derisive laughter from across the Bay.

Thankfully, those bad moments were behind. The brawling squatter towns had evolved into sedate family suburbs with dignified churches and growing academies and finishing schools. Oakland, whose population was nudging the 10,000 mark, recently had joined the ranks of modern municipalities by installing gas lights, which were lighted at dusk by a rider on horseback and extinguished at midnight. The public was supplied modern transportation in the form of narrow gauge steam railroads and streetcars pulled on rails by horses. True, the district was still plagued by streets that were appalling mud mires in winter and dust beds in summer, and Oakland sidewalks were of splintery board construction, while Alameda and Berkeley had no sidewalks at all. But urban improvements and amenities would come with the stimulus the railroad would bring, along with growth and progress.

The man who had been responsible for turning the tide — and he turned it by standing up to Nefarious Horace — was Dr. Sam Merritt. In Oakland's turbulent early history, these Yankee adversaries might be said to fill the roles of Lucifer and Guardian Angel. Dr. Merritt's aspect fitted his role no better than Carpentier's. The Maine-born doctor, who had arrived in Oakland on Halloween Day, 1854, presented a really startling vision, standing six-feet-three, weighing 340 pounds, and bristling with coal black ear-to-ear chin whiskers. At the sight of him small children cried and hid under their mothers' skirts.

But the doctor made an immediate hit in Oakland by paying cash for his land instead of squatting, and not long after became the town hero by the act of damming up the slough, making Carpentier's extortionate toll bridge superfluous. Moreover, the tract of water enclosed by the dam formed a beautiful shimmering lake. The grateful town named the tract of water after its creator,

and then elected him mayor, in which capacity he obliged them by working to stabilize property values.

The doctor's acts were not without self-interest. He had constructed the dam to enhance his vast real estate holdings, which he was rapidly multiplying by the canny scheme of offering free lumber in exchange for a mortgage, then acting quickly on foreclosures. His Oakland business ventures proved so successful he never did get around to practicing medicine, although he held a medical degree from Bowdoin College. All of the doctor's many acts of beneficence, then and later, would have a strong Merritt angle. But Victorian Era Californians highly revered business acumen, and the doctor's rising star was widely applauded.

The good doctor's most recent feat in his mayor's shoes was in forcing Carpentier to relax his hold on the Oakland water front. After much pressure, Carpentier was persuaded to cede the city a public landing and to deed the rest of the water front to a holding company in which Carpentier retained majority interest. However, the water front question would not be finally resolved until 1910, when the city, after a mountain of litigation, finally recovered the harbor which it had cheerfully presented Carpentier nearly sixty years before. Some said Dr. Merritt could have wrung more for the city than he did, for he later was found to have emerged from the negotiations with a $100,000 water front lot of his own.

Nobody could deny that the portly doctor cut a swath. He had scored socially by building himself a handsome Gothic house, the style most favored in the East Bay during its first decades of settlement. Most of the early residences built along the Oakland Estuary and along Alameda's High Street ("Old Alameda") and West End conveyed the Gothic idea in one detail or another. Moses Chase, in 1849, had become the squire of Oakland's tent village by fashioning driftwood and packing crates into a one-room cottage with a pointed roof, to which he later constructed an addition with gables, finial, and a touch of gingerbread.

But the social set Dr. Merritt was courting was building more ambitiously with the same attention to detail as in the Gothic-studded Hud-

Here lived Dr. Sam Merritt, Oakland's first citizen and frequent public servant during its pioneer decades. The ornate Italian villa and its bosky grounds occupied an entire block on Madison Street facing the lake named for the doctor, after first being called Lake Peralta. A visitor to the villa in 1881 was King Kalakaua, the royal monarch of Hawaii, who earlier had visited the doctor on his yacht in the harbor of Honolulu. The portly doctor was a lifelong bachelor; his sister acted as his hostess. (*Oakland* TRIBUNE)

son River valley at the other end of the railroad. These perpendicular, pointed houses mixed and matched such medieval features as gables and peaked roofs, finials and oriels, narrow lancet windows or arched Tudor windows, slender belfries with points or blunt ramparts with teeth. Fretwork decoration, which approximated ancient stone tracery, was moulded of terra cotta if the house were masonry, but if of wood, as were most California houses, trim was sawed gingerbread, so-called after fancy gingerbread cookies of England.

Greek Revival, which had studded the landscape with temples of every size, from banks to birdhouses, had been an excursion into the golden ages of mythology; the style revival had been sparked by the Greek archeological excavations and Lord Byron's poetry. Now the novels of Sir Walter Scott were beckoning readers into the Gothic world of knights and ladies. A Gothic house was the materialized dream of a knight riding to Camelot.

With its rustic air, Gothic looked slightly undressed without foliage; thus the style found

Snell's Seminary moved from Benicia to Oakland in 1878 and occupied this handsome Italian villa on Twelfth Street. Snell's was considered one of the most select of Oakland's several fashionable finishing schools for young ladies. Its star-struck headmistress was highly successful in ensnaring visiting artists and persuading them to perform before her girls. Flanking the Seminary on the right is the First Congregational Church. (*Albert Norman collection*)

more favor in Oakland and Alameda than in leaf-scarce San Francisco. The influential home expert Andrew Jackson Downing suggested that it be set in a "wealth of bower, vine and creeper"; and a wooded canyon behind Oakland afforded just such a setting for a Gothic mansion, which in lieu of a helmeted knight for its master had a Stetson-hatted Texas Ranger.

Wiry, piercing-eyed Colonel Jack Hays, Mexican War hero and the most spectacular Indian fighter in Texas history, had capped his career with a term as San Francisco's Vigilante sheriff before moving across the Bay. Under his high, gabled roof the Colonel now specialized in social conquests with his lavish board, which attracted guests from all over the state and further. He soon was to entertain President Grant during his California visit. At this bosky retreat, called Fernwood, (not to be confused with Fern*side*) was initiated the East Bay custom of serving abundant Sunday breakfasts to as many as a hundred guests on some occasions.

Moving dapperly in the Colonel's set was Irish-born Judge Samuel Bell McKee, who reciprocated hospitality at his more modest-sized Gothic house on Oakland's fashionable Adeline Street. The simple, subdued Gothic design had one large central gable which bisected a wide ridge roof; both eaves and gable were edged with simple scrollwork, the windows simple lancets. The judge's house rather suggested the solemnity he exuded from the bench of the county, district, and state supreme courts he successively served with distinction.

Gothic was felt to be an appropriate setting for a judge. Doting on moral principle, Victorians believed they favored Gothic for its noble qualities. In his popular book *Cottage Residences*, Downing averred that a well-designed Gothic house conveyed its owners "strong aspiration toward something higher than social pleasures." Part of its nobility, in Downing's view, lay in its lack of pretense, although Downing paradoxically suggested that when building with wood that boards be dressed to resemble stone and that paint be flecked with sand to abet the deception. Some claimed that Gothic roofs reached heavenward, as the hoary cathedrals were said to do, but in fact most Victorian Gothic roofs were not cathedral-like, but rather borrowed the slant of Alpine roofs, which being fashioned to shed snow, might be said to aim earthward. But one indubitable virtue of the Gothic house was its flexibility. Whereas the Greek Revival house rigidly ranged four-square rooms along a central hall, Gothic permitted any floor plan the heart desired; in fact, the more irregular the plan the better the opportunity to multiply the gables.

A Gothic house highly similar to Judge McKee's, situated on Oakland's East Eighteenth Street facing the Estuary, sheltered a quite different household. This shuttered Gothic cottage was one of several Oakland houses that were imported from New England in sections in the 1850s to ease the housing shortage. However, it gained its greatest claim to fame two decades later when it secluded Robert Louis Stevenson and Fanny Osbourne while they waited out her divorce from Sam Osbourne. Fanny had met Stevenson, then an unknown impecunious poet, while traveling in

Scaled for the lofty Gothic ceiling was this Gothic pipe organ, below. All manner of pointed furnishings with the appropriate upward surge were turned out to complement Gothic churches – pews, pulpits, chairs, even hymn books with pointed Gothic lettering. Gothic furniture tended to look like architecture in miniature. *(F. North collection)*

Gothic to most people suggests a church, for the Gothic Revival lasted much longer in the realm of ecclesiastical architecture. St. Paul's Episcopal Church, below, which stood at what is now Oakland's Fourteenth and Alice Streets, might be a Twentieth Century Gothic church but for its finials, striped shingle roof, and iron cresting. *(Albert Norman collection)*

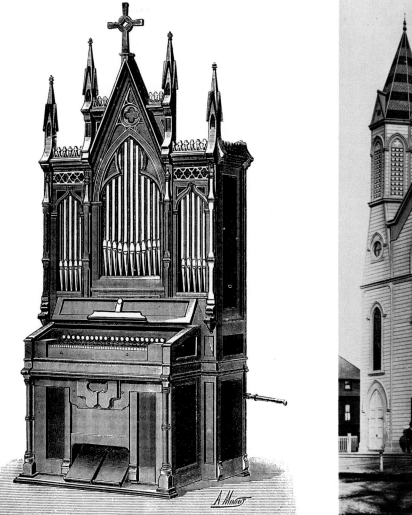

Even this horse car waiting room in East Oakland had its touch of Gothic. It much resembled the guard shelters that dotted public parks. *(Albert Norman collection)*

Europe with her daughter; she was twelve years his senior. After her return to Oakland, he followed, traveling by ship's steerage and emigrant trains. Fanny's husband Sam Osbourne, a San Francisco court stenographer, agreed to a divorce.

In the cottage on the Estuary, Stevenson worked on *Prince Otto,* the novel which would bolster his fame and his finances. Already fighting tuberculosis, he often wrote outdoors, while the diminutive, short-haired Fanny tended her flower garden. The household also included Fanny's son and daughter, her pretty younger sister, and, part of the time, Sam Osbourne. Stevenson was quite happy there and thought the cottage, then embowered with roses, a delightful abode. In the dedication to *Prince Otto,* which he completed in Europe after he and Fanny married, he affectionately described it as "far gone in the respectable stages of antiquity" so that it seemed "indissoluble from the green garden in which it stood. . . . It was a sea-traveler in its younger days, and had come around the Horn piece-meal in the belly of a ship, and might have heard the seamen stamping and shouting and the note of the boatswain's whistle."

One of Fanny's neighbors, Catherine McGrew, later added *her* comments, which are incidentally a comment on Oakland attitudes in those times: "They all lived there together, an odd Bohemian group. But they got along so well together and had such a good time . . . that we thought nothing of it."

On the same street, a more elaborate Gothic house, built in 1862, figured in another literary masterpiece. Captain Ned Wakeman, who at sea was rough and ready for the fiercest gale, when in port lived and entertained in style in his three-story showplace, modestly called Rose Cottage. The remarkably steep roof was cut by vari-sized gables airily frothed with bargeboard; it had both arched Tudor windows and slanting bays, and encircling all was a decorative veranda with split pilasters and an overhead balustrade. The fancy gate of the carved Gothic fence often swung open for the captain's journalist friend Mark Twain, who later translated his host into the redoubtable Captain Blakeley in *Roughing It.*

Dilapidated Gothic houses often have been accused of being haunted, but one East Bay Gothic mansion seemed to have harbored evil spirits from the very start. Built in the mid-1850s near the village of Brentwood, it was to have been a social coup for its owner, Dr. John Marsh, who commissioned architect Thomas Boyd to design for him the "finest house in California." Marsh specified that its dining room seat forty guests and, shrugging off earthquake warnings, he insisted his house be built of stone. He had recently married an attractive young missionary from Massachusetts and was anxious to move out of the dirt-floored adobe in which he had batched while piling up his fortune.

Whereas Dr. Merritt didn't let his medical degree steer him into a medical career, Marsh didn't let a lack of one deter him from practicing. He had arrived in California when the Mexicans still ruled, bringing only his Harvard B.A. diploma. That was all he needed, since he was able to pass it off as a medical degree to the Mexican authorities, who not only let him practice medicine but granted him a rancho of 50,000 acres near Mount Diablo. Although testy-tempered, Marsh prospered both as doctor and as cattleman, as his usual medical fee was one animal for each mile he had to travel.

A favorite mecca of the East Bay's pleasure-loving Southern set was Fernwood, the Gothic style home of Colonel Jack Hays at a site on Fish Ranch Road in Oakland's present Claremont district. The Tennessee-born colonel who was surveyor general of California, had come out as a 49er, as did other Southerners. But many were members of genteel Confederate families who came West after the Civil War to escape the carpetbaggers. *(Thompson & West's Historical Atlas of Alameda County)*

The Marsh house was a three-story cream-colored sandstone with three front-facing gables, between two of which set, perhaps at Marsh's insistence, an unharmonizing square tower, such as those on the new Italian villas going up in Oakland. The stone was quarried from the rolling mountains near the building site. That Marsh's house might have launched him socially despite its confused motif is suggested by the respectful attention it received, while still under construction, in an Oakland newspaper, which called it a "pleasant and appropriate union of manor house and castle," noting approvingly that it "has departed from the stereotyped square box . . . called a house in California." A visiting journalist termed it "the most complete private residence in California."

Then misfortune descended. The house still wasn't complete when Marsh's wife died, leaving an infant daughter. Marsh moved in, letting the third floor go unfinished, and instead of entertaining guests he spent most of his time in his 65-foot tower spying for cattle thieves with powerful field glasses — some said the tower's intended purpose. Having gathered evidence on two rustlers, he made ready to depart for San Francisco to arrange for their arrest. Before leaving he buried somewhere on the estate $5,000 in gold from a recent cattle sale.

Marsh may have been spied upon himself. His buggy was but a short distance down the road when he was waylaid and stabbed to death by three Spaniards, all said to have held grievances against the doctor. The cached gold disappeared also. One of the men was finally apprehended and brought to trial; sentenced to "life" at San Quentin, he was later pardoned. The Marsh house was occupied by others, but never grandly, and in 1868 an earthquake wracked the walls and toppled the massive tower. After that the house began to deteriorate into a spooky Gothic ruin, a lonely moldering pile, which remains today.

How was it that houses so grand as these came to be built in a place so newly-opened as the San Francisco Bay Area? After all, this was the westernmost frontier, and historically the Westward

The graceful wooden scrollwork under the steep gable of the Kelsey house at Niles is almost as delicate and lacy as the pepper tree that shades it. *(Jane Voiles collection)*

This homey Gothic church was built by Oakland's First Baptist congregation at Fourteenth and Brush Streets the same year the transcontinental railroad arrived. *(Albert Norman collection)*

---

trek had been a creeping agrarian advance, depositing dreary settlements whose make-do houses offered mere shelter from weather and coyotes and whose intellectual sustenance was limited to the almanac. What explains all the high style and creature comforts that this new citizenry demanded only a few years after James Marshall chanced upon that lump of ore at Sutter's Mill?

The difference lay in the pioneers. The gold-seekers for the most part were urban-bred sophisticates, most of them both solvent and educated. It took money and ingenuity to get around the Horn or to cross the Isthmus. Although soon after arrival they were bearded and wielding picks, they were a far cry from the homespun frontiersman and his ax. The lean-to, sheet-flapping accommodations they found in California suited

them not at all, and they promptly demanded better.

To appease their complaints, ships soon began arriving with lumber, nails and carpentry tools. Dr. Merritt had been able to buy his corner of Oakland for having had the foresight to arrive in San Francisco with a hundred kegs of nails, just after the tent town had once more expired in flames. Before he set foot on shore, the smoke assured him he could name his own price. Arriving too was the country's first pre-fab housing, partially-constructed dwellings shipped in sections from New England, Europe, and China. Alameda's first frame house was an imported French cottage.

Not far behind were trained architects. It is a little known fact that the cream of young architectural talent from all over the world was attracted by the Gold Rush. No doubt they were motivated by the same craving for the strange and distant that had inspired the romantic motifs they brought with them. Sitting before their drawing boards with prospects of serving long, spirit-curbing apprenticeships to older masters, these bright young men not only were seized by dreams of sun and gold but foresaw that all those tens of thousands debarking on California sands badly needed housing. In East Coast cities, in England, France, and Germany, they packed their T-squares and bought passage to San Francisco, bringing with them the disciplines of the American classic tradition, of the English masters, the German academies, and the French École des Beaux-Arts. After pocketing some quick money constructing at the mines, they returned to set up practice in San Francisco and Oakland and began fulfilling the dreams of a gold-richened, exuberantly optimistic society.

One can understand, then, how as early as 1864 one of these newcomers might have designed a house in Oakland that today would be pointed to by architectural scholars as exemplifying the best residential Gothic Revival architecture on the West Coast. The young architect S. H. Williams designed and supervised construction of the modest-sized (by Victorian standards) frame house popularly known today as Moss Cottage, and which has been preserved for posterity as a cultural center in Oakland's Mosswood Park.

J. Mora Moss, financier and early University of California regent (1868-1880) built the house as a middle-aged bachelor to celebrate his comeback. Moss was one of those multi-faceted Victorians who dabbled in everything. He had made and lost a fortune in Philadelphia before coming to California, and had sought out the Gold Rush to recoup. Starting out as a modest bank clerk in San Francisco, he rose to become one of the leading citizens in California. He was connected with the first telegraph system in the state and with San Francisco's first illuminating gas company. Moss also pioneered with irrigation canal building and operating and with ice-making.

Williams drew on both French and English sources for his inspiration, which is boldly romantic and elegant in detail, material, and craftsmanship. Perhaps its most dramatic feature is the roof which overhangs three feet and whose dormers project beyond the overhangs and are supported by decorative bracketry and corbels. Oriel windows, bays which both project and overhang, adorn front and side elevations. Williams gave his design an overall unity, extending Gothic detail-

After two decades of renting its city offices, Oakland built itself a handsome cupolaed city hall, the design of Sumner Bugbee. It went up in smoke less than seven years later on the night of August 25, 1877, from a blaze believed to have been purposely started with a dropped cigarette — called a cigar-reete then and only smoked by dudes. The arsonist was never found. (*Albert Norman collection*)

stairway recess, Gothic balustrade on the staircase, Gothic fireplaces, and molded cornices and molded ceiling cartouches. Its plumbing and other fixtures are typical of California domestic architecture of the 1860s. The French-style bathtub of planished tin on copper was encased in Spanish cedar; faucets were silver-plated; sink tops were of Italian marble. The clothes closets were fitted with numerous brass hooks, called "clothes pins." Pictured below is the side entrance that admits to the library-study. J. Mora Moss, a San Francisco businessman, built his house in 1863 at a site now centered at MacArthur and Broadway. In the 1860s and 1870s, many real estate tracts in the East Bay were acquired by San Franciscans for home sites or weekend cottages. In 1912, the city acquired the Moss estate at the insistence of then Mayor Frank K. Mott, to whom the park's Broadway Pergola Entrance is dedicated. *(All pictures from National Parks Service)*

"Moss Cottage," today surrounded by Oakland's Mosswood Park is a splendid example of Gothic architecture of French and English influence as adapted to wood frame. The wooden edging under the gables, called a bargeboard, is patterned after the Tudor houses of England, while the oriels, the bays projecting under the gables and supported by corbels, recall the chateaux of France. Painted green today, the exterior originally was painted white with a tinted trim that accented the dramatic scrollwork and window treatment. The architectural specifications for the house called for Gothic forms for the interior as well, including a molded Tudor arch sprung over the

At right is the interior of the Moss Cottage library-study. It has a mahogany mantel piece, mahogany book shelves, and is illuminated by stained-glass windows. Below is a detail of the intricate inside window shutters then much in use.

ing throughout the interior, to doors, fireplaces, staircases, plastic mouldings, even to the cruciform floor plan.

When his house was complete, Moss crowned his blessings with a wife, a comely New York woman who in turn crowned them with her own creation. Catching the local enthusiasm for importing foreign plants, she turned their vast grounds into an arboretum for rare trees and shrubs. So well did she select, many of them thrive today in the verdant park surrounding Moss Cottage.

The East Bay preoccupation with botany no doubt had influenced planning for the celebration that was to mark the train's four o'clock arrival. For Alamedans even surpassed Oaklanders in their zeal for encouraging the rustic aspect. Visitors exclaimed at the towering live oaks left growing in the middle of the street, at the insistence of preservationists. Indeed, Alamedans were such foliage worshipers they sometimes were accused of venerating underbrush, which they permitted to grow to obstructive heights. Some Alamedans even complained that the enthusiasm was endangering street visibility; and rattlesnakes and wood rats so abounded that boys hunted them with clubs for sport.

This Gothic house built by pioneer Dennis Straub at 2255 Pacific Avenue in Alameda would have been a century old in 1972 had it not been demolished to make way for new construction. Note its multiple gables, each lined with scrollwork bargeboard and crowned with a handsome finial of molded iron. *(Alameda Historical Society)*

Alameda's train welcoming committee had prepared a triumphal arch, the traditional **tribute** of the Romans for their returning heroes. **But** where the togaed generals and their **legions had** marched beneath a span of carven stone, **the arch** that now awaited before a freight shed down near "Cohen's Wharf" at the foot of Pacific Avenue for the historic locomotive to roll under was framed of wood and festooned with sprays of evergreen boughs and cut flowers. The blossoms, affixed only that morning, glowed in the brilliant sunshine, and to either side of the magnificent arch hung a profusion of state and national flags wafting in an occasional breeze.

As the hour of four drew near, alongside the tracks gathered a well-dressed crowd from both sides of the Bay, women in skirts belled out with crinoline, children in dark clothes and snow-white collars, frock-coated men who had closed their businesses and offices in honor of the occasion. Everybody squinted uptrack; many focused opera and field glasses.

Four o'clock came. But where was the train? The crowd began to murmur uneasily. What had happened? Wireless telegraph earlier had passed the word that the train had departed Sacramento on time, at 10 a.m. This discounted the likelihood of obstructive herds and Indians that sometimes menaced trains east of the Sierra, but in the sparsely-settled Sacramento Valley there was the possibility of desperadoes. And it was worriedly pointed out that the rails were new and untried; the last of the track — three-and-a-half miles in the vicinity of Niles — had been completed only the day before, with iron unloaded at the Alameda wharf at dawn and laid by laborers persuaded to violate the Sabbath. Could there have been an accident?

As the afternoon wore on with neither train nor explanation, the crowd began to break ranks. Depending on the train's whistle to recall them, some repaired to nearby homes and businesses, while visiting family groups fanned out to look over some of the real estate currently being promoted.

Alameda's original purchasers, William Chipman and Gideon Aughinbaugh, had paid their $14,000 for the peninsula intending to devote it to peach orchards, but their orchards soon had begun to go the way of California's later orange groves, into subdivisions (sole reminder of their orchards today is the name Peach Street). Speculators had purchased sizable tracts and were selling land at prices from $80 to $250 per lot, mostly at weekend auctions to which customers were lured over from San Francisco with the promise of free watermelon. Now the promoters were counting on the glamour of the western terminus of the transcontinental railroad to surpass watermelon as a sales lure.

One of Alameda's new subdivisions was called the Fitch Tract, after its owners the Fitch brothers, who also developed the Oakland suburb of Fitchburg. These Irish-born brothers named their streets for saints, but town fathers, predominantly Protestant, later renamed them after prominent local citizens. However, the prime attraction on the Alameda development was neither saints nor watermelon but Charles Fitch's stunning Italian villa.

This elegant new style, from which John Marsh had borrowed his tower, during the mid-1860s had overtaken Gothic as the preferred design for larger East Bay residences. Modified from Fifteenth Century Florentine palacios, and thus sometimes called Tuscan villas, these square-towered houses had such classic and baroque-classic features as columned porticos, railed balconies, roof bracketry, and arched paired windows. The roof was low, almost flat, the ground plan rectangular, or L-shaped. The villa's wide facade largely excluded it from cramped San Francisco, but the East Bay went overboard for the high, wide, and handsome houses with all the rich detailing.

Fitch's villa was quite an ornate one with several porticos and balconies and with scarcely any of its long paired windows exactly alike. Both its roof and its tower wore frilly iron cresting. A large stable had its own rococo tower too, while the decorated water tower seemed to imitate a Tuscan campanile. The extensive grounds with formal landscaping were cut by three walks, each leading to its own fancy gateway through the ornate iron fence.

The Italian style had received a big assist from Dr. Merritt. In 1863, the lake he had enclosed had so enhanced his real estate, he was able to exchange his Gothic house for a mansion-sized Italian villa, which he constructed on a choice lake-front site. His magnificent example precipitated a rash of adjacent villa-building which further enhanced his holdings. The doctor's villa, like himself, had its unconventionalities. It substituted columned windows with pediments for the simpler arched ones; it had a French mansard roof; and instead of one tower, it had two, a square one at one end, an octagonal one at the other. Architects often took liberties with these towers, giving them various placements. If the plan were rectangular, the tower might be set front-center, or at one end, or one at each end; if the plan were L-shaped, the tower was placed at the turn. Or the tower might be centered atop the house, like the pinnacle on a tureen cover, in which case it was called a cupola.

California towers were equally versatile in use. Ranchers, like Marsh, found watching their herds through field glasses from a tower easier than riding the range; captains and fleet owners climbed into towers to observe their ships in the harbor; ministers used them for composing sermons; some owners used them as air-conditioned billiard rooms.

One of Oakland's first Italian villas became famed for still another activity in its cupola. It

Oakland and San Francisco Time Table.

Leave San Francisco.		Leave Oakland.	
A. M.	P. M.	A. M.	P. M.
†6.10	*12.30	†5.20	*12.20
7.00	1.00	†6.00	12.50
7.30	*1.30	6.50	*1.20
8.00	2.00	7.20	*1.35
8.30	3.00	7.50	†1.50
9.00	3.30	8.25	2.50
9.30	4.00	8.50	3 20
10.00	4.30	9.20	3.50
*10.30	5.00	9.50	4.20
11.00	5.30	*1020	4.50
*11.30	6.00	10.50	5.20
12.00	6.30	*11.20	5.50
	7.00	11.50	6.30
	§8.10		6.50
	9.20		7.20
	10.30		8.00
	†11.45		9.10
			10 20

*—Sundays only.   †—Except Sundays.

The clatter of hammers constructing the four-story Grand Central Hotel in central Oakland forecast the era of prosperity that was generated by the transcontinental railroad. The impressive structure was the design of Dr. Sam Merritt, Oakland booster extraordinary, who financed half of its $200,000 cost and personally selected much of its plush furnishings that included 2800 yards of Axminster and Brussels carpeting and rosewood and mahogany furniture. Boasted the Oakland *Transcript:* "Oakland eclipses the big city on the wrong side of the Bay so far as her hotel accommodations are concerned." Its dining room was popular with San Franciscans. The menu, shown at left, included the schedules of the Oakland and San Francisco Railroad's ferry service. It was a subtle reminder of how convenient it was to cross the Bay and enjoy the Grand Central's excellent cuisine. *(Albert Norman collection)*

44

Table d' Hote.

Saturday, May 20th, 1876.

Soup.

Ox Tail, a la Anglaise,   Clear Julienne.

Fish.

Boiled California Blue Cod, Parsley Sau

Cold.

Ham,   Veal.

Boiled.

Leg of Mutton, Caper Sauce,   Whitaker's Ham,   Corned Beef and Cabbage.
                                Tongue.

Roasts.

Rib Beef,   Mutton   Ham, Champagne Sauce.
        Lamb, Mint Sauce.   Loin of Mutton, Currant Jelly,

Entrees.

Rabbit Saute, a la Chesseur,
        Fricassee, a la Rhine,
                Ris de Veau Pique, au Champignons,
                        Langue de Mutton Garned, au Petite Poise,
                                Fillet of Beef, Saute, a la Bordeiaise,
                                        Maccaroni, with Ham and Cheese

Vegetables.

Boiled Potatoes,   Lima Beans.   Mashed Potatoe.
        Cabbage,   Green Corn,   Parsnips,
        Beets,   Cauliflower,   Rice,

Relishes.

Yorkshire Sauce,   French Mustard.
Assorted Pickles.   Olives,   Nabob Sauce
        Pickled Beets,   Worcestershire Sauce,

Pastry.

Apple Pies,   Cabinet Pudding, wine Sauce,   Green Gage Pies.

Confectionery.

Wine Cake,   Drop Cakes,   Citron Drops,
                            Cocoanut Cakes,

Dessert.

Green and Black Tea,   English Walnuts
        French Coffee,   Oranges   Malaga Raisins
                Apples,   Almonds
                Filberts,   Pecans,
                        Pine Apple Ice Cream.

The Lines of the Western Union Telegraph Company connect with the House.

HOURS OF MEALS.

BREAKFAST—From 7 to 11.   LUNCH—From 12.30 to 2.30.
DINNER—From 5 to 7.   SUPPER—From 7.20 to 9.

SUNDAYS.

BREAKFAST—From 8 to 11.   LUNCH—From 1 to 2.30.
DINNER—From 5 to 7.   SUPPER—From 7.30 to 9.

NURSES AND CHILDREN.

BREAKFAST—7.   LUNCH—12   DINNER—5.

Meals in Rooms, Lunches and Fruits Charged extra.

The Grand Central's Table d'Hote featured eleven courses, most with multiple choices. Like most pretentious hotels of the day, it printed its entrees in French, and served nurses and children separately. Western Union Telegraph service was available right in the hotel.

(F. North collection)

45

Above is a sketch of the College of California, predecessor of the University of California, in the 1860s, when it was comprised of only two buildings. Both were in the then popular Italian Villa style. The leafy campus covered four blocks bounded by Twelfth, Fourteenth, Franklin and Harrison Streets, now the heart of Oakland's business district. After the College became the University and moved to Berkeley in 1873, College Hall was converted to quite a different use — that of a livery stable, shown at right. (*Albert Norman collection*)

was a low, modest-sized square villa of a rare (for California) lathe and plaster construction, the first in Oakland; it had long, shuttered windows and an encircling veranda. Its builder was a pioneer from upstate New York, Colonel Andrew Williams, who had sided with Dr. Merritt against Carpentier and during the 1860s served two terms as Oakland's mayor. Colonel Williams built it for his bride, a New York widow who came west with a teenage son and daughter. Behind the glistening white plaster of the house, which stood at Fifth and Clay Streets, was said to be a framework made of drygoods packing boxes.

The Colonel's stepson, a dreamy youth, soon appropriated the cupola for composing poetry and for entertaining friends who also courted the muse — Oakland's first literary coterie. The young man made pocket money tutoring and clerking in a drugstore until he started selling stories under the name of Bret Harte. His famous tale "The Luck of Roaring Camp," based on his experiences in the Sierra gold country, is said to have been written in the cupola. So inspirational did he find the cupola that even after he published *Bohemian Days* and could afford his own flat, the budding author continued to write in the Williams' cupola. He did, that is, until Colonel Williams had the bad luck of having his title challenged by an early squatter. He fought hard in the courts, but in the end he lost his lot, his villa, and Bret Harte's writing studio.

The Italian villa style had an earlier association with poetry. The Italy-flavored poems of Robert and Elizabeth Browning did much to popularize the style in England, after those most romantic of all Victorians fled England, more specifically fled the thunder of Elizabeth's high Victorian father. When they took refuge in Florence, a Florentine craze swept England like a maddening mistral, prompting large numbers to hie to Florence and become Browning-watchers. Those compelled to remain behind in foggy England could nourish their dreams with Florentine engravings and art objects and especially by living in a Tuscan villa. The style was cinched when Victoria and Albert, those second-most romantic Victorians, commissioned their villa Osborne on the Isle of Wight. From England the style spread to the American Eastern Seaboard, then around the Horn to California. Unlike Gothic, Italian villas never caught on in the Midwest.

One home manual editor recommended Italian villas for "clear and sunny glades." A prepossessing villa recently had been erected at an Oakland site chosen because it was the sunniest place its owner could find. Dr. Enoch Homer Pardee had come across the Bay from San Francisco seeking warmth, and when he came upon a lot in San Pablo bathed in brilliant sunshine he bought it on the spot, only to learn its characteristic fog had but momentarily lifted. He posted it for sale and began a more cautious search, finally deciding on a lot near the Oakland water front that had been a basking place for ducks and seagulls.

The young Rochester-born physician, who had earned a $15,000 nest egg panning gold before setting up practice in San Francisco, built a beautifully-proportioned villa that was destined to become one of the most important social centers of California. Later he was to serve Oakland as mayor and in other important public capacities, as would his physician son Dr. George C. Pardee, who would occupy the villa after his term as California's efficient "Earthquake Governor."

The villa entrance was most impressive with its expertly-wrought Corinthian columned and pilastered portico, above which, at the second-story roof level, arched a classic pediment. A smaller pediment was repeated on the central square tower, and miniature pediments echoed over the long arched double windows. The cornice departed from the classic correctness of the portico; regular modillions (classic brackets) were spaced by elongated console brackets. Another style departure was the slanted bays on side elevations.

Like nearly all California villas, the Pardee house was built of wood, in this case redwood, instead of the brick or stone generally used in the East. California carpenters became skilled at the translation, scoring the edges of wide horizontal boards to make them resemble fitted stone slabs and fitting wooden blocks at corners to simulate stone support quoins. Local planing mills supplied the rounded arches and carved mouldings and modillions. Sometimes pediments enclosed wood panels carved to resemble etched stone entablatures. The Pardee house, copying the color scheme of Eastern villas, originally was

This notable example of the Italian Villa style at 672 Eleventh Street in Oakland was for decades an important social center, successively the home of the eminent Pardees, Enoch H. and George C. Both were prominent physicians, both Oakland mayors, and the latter served as California governor and was first to occupy the governor's mansion after its acquisition by the state. This well-preserved house not only retains its original landscaping, water tower, carriage house and stables, but is still occupied by members of the Pardee family. (*National Parks Service*)

painted a sand-grey with the corner quoins painted brick-red.

Some architecture critics of the day professed to sternly disapprove of these painstaking deceptions, one complaining of "such fantastic tricks before high Heaven as make the angels weep." But Californians delighted in their "fool the eye" facsimiles, and such houses as the Pardees' were much admired and imitated. That the house and its sunny glade pleased the Pardees is indicated by the fact that it has since been Pardee-occupied. The present occupants are the Misses Helen and Madeline Pardee, daughters of Dr. George, who have immaculately maintained the house, now painted white, as well as the original carriage house, stable and tank house. They as carefully preserve the formal landscaping, replacing each departed shrub with its exact replica. This house on Oakland's Eleventh Street is probably the best-preserved early Victorian in California.

Two other future East Bay politicos chose the Italian villa style. In Alameda, Henry H. Haight, then in Sacramento in the governor's mansion, had built a handsome villa with central cupola and pedimented windows. Its large garden with its fountains and grass terraces was the scene of many outdoor functions.

Not far from the Pardees', genial, full-mustachioed N. W. Spaulding, also to serve as Oakland's mayor, built a splendid villa with earnings from operating a hotel and sawmill at the Calaveras County diggings. This Maine-born native also would serve as the first master of the Masonic Lodge of Oakland. The house, whose showy roof was capped with a finialed cupola and edged with iron cresting, was situated in a formally-landscaped block through which carriage drives curved to two imposing entrances on opposite sides of the almost square villa. Each columned entrance admitted to a spacious entrance hall paved with black and white marble laid in a domino pattern.

As they did in England, villas found rural favor in California. Two famous agriculturists chose the style for their homes on farms behind Oakland. America's first sugar beets yielded the fortune that built the Ebenezer H. Dyer villa near Alvarado, an elegant rectangular mansion with a sizable front-centered tower that resembled the Giralda in Seville. Convinced the locale possessed a suitable climate for cultivating sugar beets, Maine-born Dyer, in the early 1860s, gambled a sizable investment in planting beets and establishing a sugar mill. At first the industry faltered, then caught on, and by 1869 Dyer was able to build a villa suitable for an affluent country squire.

Near Hayward, amidst vast orchards and berry fields, William Meek cultivated a ten-acre formal garden of imported trees and shrubs and a high-gushing Italian fountain set in a lily pond. Dominating all this splendor was a nineteen-room villa in which Italian details mingled with two features of an incoming French style, *Oeil de boeuf* windows and the mansard roof which capped the square tower.

Meek pioneered the fruit industry in the West, after bringing out the first grafted fruit trees to Oregon in a covered wagon over the Oregon Trail. Shifting his nursery business from Oregon to Alameda County, there he developed the Royal Anne and Bing cherries, the latter named for his Chinese cook. In addition to his cherries, Meek's memory is perpetuated by his charming villa and gardens, which the city of Hayward has preserved (and opens daily) for public enjoyment.

Another, quite different architectural style probably attracted interest and comment among visitors to Alameda on that September afternoon in 1869. Rarely seen in San Francisco, the so-called Mother Lode style was favored by a scattering of East Bay residents, especially Forty-Niners who had met some luck in the gold fields, where the motif evolved. Carpenters there had given simple ridge-roofed New England-type houses an encircling Spanish veranda, which the miners called a gallery. The gallery was dressed up with turned pilasters and balustrades and other frills from the planing mills. In 1965, an admirer of one such surviving house in Alameda purchased it to save it from being demolished and was delighted to find one room furnished like a miner's cabin, complete with supply of gold dust bags.

✓   ✓   ✓

The transcontinental train did eventually arrive that day, but not until nearly ten p.m. No disaster had occurred, merely a series of minor

49

but persistent interruptions. After the train clanged out of Sacramento, crowded with free riders invited aboard to fill empty seats, there had been one exasperating delay after another. Repeatedly the train had had to halt before squatting construction crews making final rail connections, and at several towns the engineer felt obliged to halt for band-playing, flag-waving celebrations. During one celebration stop a well-wisher had fired a cannon improperly, shattering the windows on one side of the train, terrifying passengers already edgy from a week of bone-jarring locomotion. This delayed departure until glass could be removed and passengers soothed.

Complication had reached a crescendo at the San Joaquin River. There a bridge tender with one eye cocked for the overdue train had fouled up the mechanism while permitting a boat to pass, and when the train arrived the span stood adamantly upended before the scowling cowcatcher. This impasse lasted more than four hours, during which the sun set and passengers dourly reflected that had they taken a river boat they might be dining in San Francisco.

Then suddenly the drawbridge went down and the river was behind and the train was clacking through the darkness along the well-oiled San Francisco & Alameda line, making up time and whistling warnings of its coming. The train came hurtling into Alameda, belching fire and smoke from its bonnet stacks and announcing its arrival with triumphant bell-ringing. It clacked on through the dark town (Alameda still lacked street lights) and entered the Pacific Avenue ferry slip on San Francisco Bay.

There a faithful crowd waited still by lantern light, diminished in size, but not in spirit. Ecstatically they cheered and waved and jumped for joy. As the engine puffed under a somewhat wilted triumphal arch, someone fired a cannon, quite properly, and everybody pressed forward to touch and caress the history-making train consisting of three linked wood-burning locomotives pulling twelve skinny frame coaches, which bore, somewhere amongst the throng of whooping freeloaders, eleven weary overland passengers.

As chronicled the following day in the San Francisco *Alta Californian* (whose reporter may have lost his note pad in the excitement, and so was obliged to substitute lyricism for details): "The noise of the bells, and boys, and men all made a conglomerate language which would set at bay the untiring genius of modern philology . . . every heart that could scan the past and survey the future filled with emotion as the spectre of fire and life came . . ."

Survey the future they could, indeed! Though the run from Sacramento had taken four hours longer than the river boat and six hours longer than the stage, the first transcontinental train had arrived at San Francisco Bay, and the East Bay indubitably had arrived in California.

Built by William Meek, who pioneered the fruit industry in the West, this Italian Villa in Hayward is an elegant survivor from the 1860s — but it had a narrow escape. When a purchaser announced his intention to raze it and turn the site to apartment development, a citizen's committee rallied strongly to its defense and waged a campaign that persuaded the city to purchase the house and its extensive gardens. Now open daily for public enjoyment, the Meek estate is one of the prides of Hayward. (*Oakland* Tribune)

North Hall, in the French mansard style, was one of the first two buildings to be constructed on the Berkeley campus of the University of California. In July, 1873, it was the setting of two kinds of commencement exercises: ceremonies marking the removal of the University from Oakland to Berkeley and the first graduation exercises on the Berkeley campus. After completing work for their degrees on the Oakland campus, students marched in body to the newly-completed building to receive their diplomas. Handsome South Hall, below, was the other new building; recently restored, it is serving well today. When the campus was transferred, Berkeley was a tiny and distant settlement and its selection as the campus site was highly controversial. Typical of the criticism was this bluster from General Barton S. Alexander: "Not anything within cannon shot of you! You might as well be on the top of the Sierra Nevada Mountains. The truth is the University ought to have been in this city (San Francisco)." But a decade later, the Oakland *Enquirer* could confidently boast: "The East Bay is the educational center of California and the Pacific Coast." (*Berkeley Firefighters Association and Bancroft Library*)

The Lotus Eaters

To the mere bystander, the University of California commencement procession that set out from Oakland for Berkeley in mid-morning on July 16, 1873, may not have worn the air of a historical event. Leading was nearly a score of leisurely-rumbling open carriages bearing mortarboarded faculty members and top-hatted dignitaries; among them was Governor Newton Booth, the former keeper of a Sacramento general store, who was running for United States Senator. Following in their dust and wheel tracks was a brisk-marching contingent that included three strutting drum majors, twelve black-suited-and-vested baccalaureate candidates, almost the entire student body in uniform (147 registered that year), several dozen friends and relatives, and a straggle of small boys and frisking dogs.

However, most members of the procession were importantly aware of its significance. The twelve dark-garbed young men comprised the first graduating class that the young and struggling University had produced. Furthermore, the exercises to so annoint them would signify the opening of the new Berkeley campus — so new, in fact, that carpenters and masons were still working on the first two buildings. Since its metamorphosis five years before from the private College of California, the University had been cramped in Oakland's booming, distracting downtown, and the administration was most anxious to shift its scholars to quieter groves of academe.

The summer sun grew hotter and the route along then Telegraph Road, so-called for its telegraph line, became increasingly rutted and dusty, but the procession's good humor was indomitable. The new Berkeley campus no longer was a probability, but a rising reality. After exasperatingly stalling and hedging on promises to construct the new campus, even threatening to abandon the Berkeley site in favor of San Francisco, the state finally had come through with two handsome modern buildings — North Hall and South Hall. Architect David Farquharson had designed both structures in dark red brick with grey stone trim and had capped them with fashionable French mansard roofs; interiors glistened with varnished hardwoods and curvaceous millwork. Such splendid buildings surely signified permanence; there would be no pulling the Berkeley site out from under *them*.

Obtaining shelter had been one of the school's most plaguing problems from its earliest beginnings, as one of the dignitaries riding ahead could well attest. Dr. Henry Durant, a Yale-educated Massachusetts minister, had come West in 1853 seeking, not gold, but to start a school. He had done so forthwith in Oakland, almost miraculously, during the height of the squatter-jumper period. California Congregationalists and Presbyterians, especially Dr. Samuel Hopkins Willey, a Dartmouth graduate, had encouraged Dr. Durant in his educational project, but they were power-

53

less to help him cope with Oakland's desperate housing shortage.

The only shelter available in the roistering squatter town was a vacated fandango house, and it was a measure of the doctor's pedagogic dedication that he consented to occupy it. Rechristening it the Contra Costa Academy, which he termed a "family high school for boys," he opened classes June 20, 1853, with three pupils.

But the premises were to suffer still further degradation. When Dr. Durant ran out of operating money, the couple he had engaged as caretaker and housekeeper undertook to recoup unpaid wages by surreptitiously operating a saloon in a corner of the building. Dr. Durant discovered it and, putting aside temptations to cloak this scandal that might sully his school, he called in the law to deal with Oakland's first speak-easy.

Anxious to remove his students from the aura of fandango and saloon, Dr. Durant did in Oakland what he would never have done in Boston; after selecting a lot he deemed appropriate for his school site (Spanish-owned, of course), he squatted upon it. More exactly, he enclosed it with a strong metal fence financed by San Francisco well-wishers. Then he contracted for a new school to be constructed, hopefully with a building fund he was soliciting in the East.

However, Eastern donations proved disappointing (Dr. Durant encountered the attitude that California was already bountifully supplied with gold), and he ran out of funds again. Construction had to be halted. When he learned that the unpaid contractor was seeking to get possession of the house by obtaining a lien, he moved into the partially-built structure by night and retired with an ax lying beside him. Alerted of the doctor's move, the contractor entered with two burly fellows, intent on carrying out an unceremonious eviction. But whether impressed by the doctor's righteous indignation or by his ax, the contractor retreated and agreed to extend time to meet the payments.

The resolute doctor met them, and the building was completed and reoccupied, this time with dignity. The academy in time grew into a college, as the doctor, doggedly continuing his fund-raising bolstered both his faculty and his facilities. Over two decades, the land he audaciously had fenced in acquired a cluster of attractive buildings, designed variously in Gothic, Italian villa, and French styles. In time the doctor was able to occupy a modest-sized Italian villa with cupola that stood on the present site of the Oakland *Tribune*. Yet, financial difficulty pursued the school throughout its Oakland period, and at one time students were obliged to make door-to-door solicitations to save their school bell from being repossessed by a San Francisco hardware firm. A portrait photographer of the time caught Dr. Durant in a characteristic pose, sitting bolt upright with tight lips and a clenched fist.

On Commencement Day, 1873, the doctor's thinning hair and side "weepers" were streaked with gray. It was with relief that, after serving as the University's first president, he was now retired. Thus he, at least, could philosophically view the school's latest scandal: accusations of graft and excessive profits in the construction of North Hall were being investigated by the state legislature. From the perspective of experience, the battle-scarred founder knew serenely that "This too will pass."

Despite its incongruous setting — those elegant buildings rising, like a mirage, from stubby, brown fields but recently diverted from grain cultivation — that first Berkeley commencement was an impressive one. History triumphed over the aroma of graft and wet mortar as President Daniel Coit Gilman (soon to found Johns Hopkins University) presented ribbon-tied diplomas to twelve young men glowing with California zest after a two-hour hike. He informed them that besides being artium baccalaurei, they were twelve "apostles" — which appellation they seemed to have accepted with profound gravity. Collectively, they would supply California with a congressman, a governor, a University regent, two University professors, three lawyers, two financiers, and one minister. One apostle, Oaklander Clarence Wetmore, doubly famed as the first student to register at the University, would give a boost to one of the state's newest industries by establishing the Cresta Blanca Winery.

Later in the day, Governor Booth made the official announcement that the University had "taken possession of its permanent site in Berkeley where it looks down upon a busy highway of

"Hay Burners" provided the only public transportation between Oakland and Berkeley during the University's early days. The trip lasted an hour-and-a-half. The decades of the Seventies and Eighties may be termed the era of the horsecars, for they provided the local linkages necessary for the expansion of the East Bay. Plush, extra-fare double-deckers were placed in service, so ladies might ride above the tobacco smoke and coarse talk of male passengers. Horsecars could be rented for weddings and picnics. Oakland even had a black-curtained horsecar hearse. *(Louis Stein collection)*

nations and is kept cool and pure by the salt sea breezes of a limitless ocean."

Significantly, the governor had mentioned the view *from* Berkeley, instead of the view *of*. Berkeley, a village of scarcely five hundred souls, hadn't much to look at, and most of what it had was located down near the water front in West Berkeley. There small residences and businesses were clustered along present San Pablo Avenue near a dock served by a ferry that ran to San Francisco. West Berkeley wasn't overly neighborly with the University set. Berkeley long would be troubled by this geographical division, which caused progress-hindering jealousies and squabbles between the east and west communities.

The indubitable proof that the University actually was moving to Berkeley lent encouragement to civic improvements already hesitantly underway in the University community. Town fathers, envisioning a college town like Harvard's Cambridge, were dangling building lots at "gentlemen of influence" inviting them to "establish a society famed for its culture and refinements." Thus imbued, they had named Berkeley after the Irish poet-philosopher Bishop George Berkeley

who had authored a much-admired poem beginning, "Westward the course of empire takes its way." (At first some confused him with Colonial Virginia's Governor Berkeley, notorious for opposing public education and free speech.) The town had adopted a system of literary ways and scientific streets, named after noted scientists and authors. Recently the University regents had commissioned the eminent New York landscape architect Frederick Law Olmsted to lay out the barren hillside campus.

Although on Commencement Day these learned streets were less visible than the cow paths that mazed Berkeley's grassy slopes, soon thereafter road workers began raising dust in earnest. Attractive faculty homes began rising between the scattered homes of ranchers and villagers. Dr. Willey, who had helped Dr. Durant found the academy, already had built a handsome town house on a foothill estate near present Dwight Way and College Avenue; in his home was formed Berkeley's first city government. Napoleon Bonaparte Byrne, who had arrived from Missouri by covered wagon in 1859 after freeing his slaves, in 1868 had built a handsome mansion, "The Cedars," on the south bank of Cordonices Creek. One of Berkeley's first American settlers, Francis Kittredge Shattuck, who was swiftly piling up a fortune invested in a stage line, livery stable, paper mill, and coal mine, recently had built a handsome mansarded house, locating it where Hinks Department Store stands today. Many of the new homes built by the incoming "gentlemen of influence" and by the University faculty were crowned with French mansard roofs, echoing the motif of the new campus buildings.

Emerging too were new commercial structures, including a hotel and a French restaurant, most of these concentrated south of the campus around the end of the horsecar line to Oakland. The horsecar was Berkeley's sole mode of public transportation, but for a stage that ran along present San Pablo Avenue to the landing in West Berkeley.

After Commencement Day, Berkeley assumed a growth rate faster than any other municipality in the state. Yet, incorporation would have to wait until 1878, largely due to those east-west disputes, and the town would long remain short on urban amenities, such as transportation, utilities, and sidewalks. Berkeley's early image was a rather startling blend of elegance and untamed nature, appealing in some ways, trying in others, especially during the rainy season. Possibly for that reason the comparison to urbane Cambridge was quietly dropped and analogy made instead to ancient Athens, which also had cerebrated without benefit of street lights or rapid transit. Berkeleyans began calling their town "The Athens of the West."

In its enthusiasm for the French mansard, or Second Empire, style, Berkeley was merely keeping abreast of international fashion. Infatuation with the court styles of the first Napoleon Bonaparte's nephew, Napoleon III, and his ravishing Empress Eugenie palpitated throughout Europe and North and South America, but nowhere more fervently than in California.

Food, furnishing, and architecture were speaking French. Women affected the empress' shorter, tighter skirts, and had their milliners copy her little coquettish hats. And everybody was dropping French phrases to the best of his ability. The architectural style that Napoleon had decreed for

This was the front of the catalogue Watts issued in advertising the auction of the Watts Tract; it tells its own eloquent story.

New suburban tracts and subdivisions popped up along the horsecar routes. A car line that extended from Oakland along San Pablo opened up new developments in West Berkeley. (*Oakland Public Library*)

Paris — the motif of the Paris Opera House and the new additions to the Louvre — was echoed in mansions on New York's Fifth Avenue, in the palaces of the silver and railroad nabobs on Nob Hill, and in mansions and public buildings rising throughout the growing East Bay. No matter that by 1873 the ebullient French monarchs had been bounced into exile in England, the Parisian craze was still in high gear, and in Northern California, at least, its momentum would carry it well into the 1880s.

The style's most salient feature was the mansard roof, a high, broken-sloped roof whose lower

56

Mark Twain with mustache and plug hat stands sampling the supposedly beneficial pink sulphur water that bubbled in the Bushy Dell near the Piedmont Springs Hotel. Then a roving journalist for mine country newspapers, Twain was a frequent visitor to the East Bay. The Piedmont hotel with its beautiful grounds was a popular place to drive to for dining or to quaff a few at the bar. But residents of the budding suburb complained of rowdiness on the premises and tried to get the hotel's liquor license revoked, without success. Piedmonters were rather relieved when the hotel burned to the ground on a New Year's Day in the late 1880s. (*Bancroft Library*)

slope approached the vertical. Windows perforated the lower roof, either dormers or round *Oeil de boeuf* openings. These eccentric roofs evolved as a tax-evasion scheme in the Seventeenth Century, when a Frenchman's tax bill depended on the number of floors; by wedging one floor under his roof and cutting windows through he also cut his bill. But by the time of Napoleon III, the roof served mere fancy and usually wore a frivolous iron crest. Facade features included long paired windows, grilled balconies, and recessed fanlighted entrances with columns and broken pediments. The French Consul to San Francisco built such a Parisian mansion in brick that was much admired and widely copied on both sides of the Bay. W. K. Brackett built one derivative on Ala-

meda's wide, posh Grand Avenue; constructed of wood dressed to resemble stone, it was a much-admired showplace then, and remains one today, having been expertly restored by Hubbard Moffitt, Jr., in the 1940s.

Many East Bay mansards departed from this neat composition. It was at this time that Bay Area architects and builders, catching the heady individualism in the air, began to improvise, mixing styles, experimenting with form, and inventing details. Mansards were blithely wedded to Italian details, to bay windows, to verandas, even to Gothic gingerbread. Needless to say, the success of these matches varied with the skill of the matchmaker. Architects even took liberties with the mansard roof itself; instead of sloping it

57

The favorite Victorian of many Oaklanders is this house built by the Boyd Family in 1871 at 370 Thirty-Fourth Street, when the street was named Plymouth. William M. Boyd, a New Englander, was an executive with Folger & Company, coffee merchants. Later the residence was occupied by Boyd family connections, the Harry Benner fam- ily. The windows of this charming mansarded house cut into the roof line. All mansard roofs had a double pitch, but their variety was almost endless. While the space under a peaked roof is a cramped tunnel, the top floor of a mansarded house is quite livable. *(Jane Voiles collection)*

straight, the builder might shape it concave or convex, or twist it into an exuberant S-shape.

One extant Oakland mansard has still another variation. Built by the Boyd family in 1871 at a location north of the corporate limits then called Seminary Hill because of its schools and today called Pill Hill for its hospitals, the house has a shuttered, octagon-shaped facade whose second- story windows extend their arched tops into the roof line, thus giving the effect of a scalloped night cap.

One of the East Bay's most striking mansard residences, both in appearance and in reputation, was a commodious verandaed mansion built in 1869 in the fashionable residential district border- ing Lake Merritt. Its vast concave roof had a startling pattern of striped shingles in contrasting colors, this topped by a high, serrated cresting. Fanning out from the residence was a children's playhouse, billiards house, and carriage house, each with its striped and crested mansard.

But the house was best known for its jinx. Its builder never got to occupy it; he went bankrupt during its construction. It was bought in 1872 by James Latham, wealthy stockbroker brother of Governor (and later Senator) Milton Latham. Three years later, Latham died on a steamer crossing the Atlantic. His widow sold to Hugh Glenn, millionaire wheat grower known as the "wheat king" for whom Glenn County was named. Fif-

teen months later Glenn was murdered by a dismissed employee. The house then sold to Horace Seaton, nephew and business partner of Collis P. Huntington. Four years later Seaton died of a heart attack.

But after years of being called the "jinx house," early in this century it came to be pointed out pridefully as the boyhood home of Scott Seaton, Horace's son, who had become a famous stage actor. Shaking the jinx, Scott Seaton carried his success into the screen and television eras and good health into his nineties.

Mansards capped most of Oakland's new public and institutional buildings during the 1870s.

The French-style D. Henshaw Ward house, below, once stood on the present site of the Lake Merritt Hotel. This 1883 mansion was typical of the grand estates that comprised the residential district that bordered Lake Merritt. They had immaculate grassy lawns that stretched down to the water's edge, where nearly every family had its own private boathouse. One Oaklander recalls the district as it appeared when he worked as a messenger boy in the area: "There was always an air of charm and good living about those homes. My boyhood hopes would drift into dreams of the day I'd be rich and famous and live in such a house and have carriages and horses in the barn and a croquet set on the lawn." (*Albert Norman collection*)

One was the second Oakland City Hall (the first was rented offices over shops), a handsome classic-detailed building with an ornate clock tower, designed by the Canadian-born architect Sumner Bugbee; the much-admired building was only seven years old when it burned at the hands of a political incendiarist. Its replacement was a more economical design. Mills Seminary, forerunner of the college, upon transferring its operation to Oakland from Benicia in 1871, moved into a long, four-story building with a high central observatory. The mansarded structure, which provided homes for faculty and students as well as classrooms and dining halls, long was considered the most beautiful educational building in the state. Oakland's first high school building was a three-story mansarded frame with tower. The tower of the new First Congregational Church on Clay Street was topped with an elongated mansard roof.

Also strikingly mansarded was the block-square Tubbs Hotel, which opened with fanfare in 1870, to vie with San Francisco's Palace Hotel in both splendor and service. Its owner Hiram Tubbs occupied an opulent mansarded mansion across the street. Public entertainment, in the form of dancing and dining out, was coming into its own, and the Tubbs quickly became an East Bay social center. Dinner every night was full dress. After moving to Oakland from Pennsylvania, the Donald Stein family, whose two younger members were Gertrude and Leo, lived there a year, before acquiring a large frame house in East Oakland. Robert Louis Stevenson stayed at the Tubbs when he first came to Oakland to be near Fanny Osborne.

The Tubbs Hotel made national news in 1879 when it was the setting of a reception for President Ulysses S. Grant, hosted by Colonel Jack Hays and other prominent East Bay figures. While in Oakland, the general visited with his son Jesse Grant and family at their home in the new suburb of Piedmont.

The real estate boom that had blossomed in Berkeley in the early 1870s coincided with a general acceleration throughout the East Bay. After the railroad arrived, homes began going up in such volume that the population would triple

within six years. Optimism was soaring so high that some predicted that Oakland would eclipse San Francisco because of its strategic advantages. These now included both a deep-water wharf and the terminal to the transcontinental railroad.

The decision of the Central Pacific to shift its terminal from Alameda to Oakland to take advantage of the new wharf was deeply disappointing to Alamedans. However, Alameda's quieter, more pastoral setting was attracting those newcomers who feared Oakland was growing too urban. Some prospering Alameda realtors were saying "good riddance" to the stir the terminal had kicked up during its brief stay. However, to tap some of the benefits of Oakland's commercial development, Alameda, in 1871, constructed a new road and bridge that connected the peninsula to Oakland's bustling downtown. A short stage line was introduced along this new route.

Oakland, of course, was highly pleased to get the railroad terminal, and for the day the shift was made, town fathers had planned a celebration calculated to eclipse the one Alameda had held. But through mixed cues, the transcontinental train arrived in Oakland an hour early, before the welcomers had gathered at the station around the triumphal arch copied after Alameda's. Worse, the train paused but momentarily under the arch before rolling prosaically on to the Oakland ferry wharf.

Oakland sighed over its marred ceremony, complaining that it never had had luck with welcoming celebrations. The one planned for the arrival of the first Pony Express, in 1860, had been spoiled by an irreverent college boy who had masqueraded as the brave rider and come galloping into town with phony saddlebags. He quite stole

---

The impressive mansarded James Latham house is seen behind a row of palms. (*Jane Voiles collection*)

"This was the era of the great popularity of everything French . . . There was such a passion for the French fashion of face enameling, as it was called, and hair dying, and padding and puffing the convexities of the human form, that preachers again thundered Cotton-Matherishly from their pulpits, and editors blasted from their presses, and husbands railed from their breakfast-and-supper-table rostra, and small boys taunted from their lamppost perches." — *Julia Cooley Altrocchi*

Oakland's Tubbs Hotel during the 1870s was one of the most elegant hotels in California. Hiram Tubbs built it after making a fortune in the cordage business and on investments in Comstock Lode silver stock, and he designed its service to attract the financial giants of the region. They lined the great mahogany bar for aperitifs and, after a gourmet dinner, spent the evening at baize-covered poker tables, winning and losing fortunes. The hotel was the scene of a gargantuan banquet held on July 4, 1876, commemorating the one-hundredth anniversary of American independence. *(Albert Norman collection)*

Oakland dearly loved a public celebration, especially those on the Fourth of July. Soldiers were invited from the Presidio and other government posts to come and join the grand parade. For the occasion, all societies, posts, clubs and public buildings in the line of march decked themselves with flags and bunting. At right in its holiday decor is Oakland City Hall — the one built in 1877 to replace the hall that burned. After the big parade, there would be lengthy speeches and "literary exercises." The day ended with splendid fireworks on Lake Merritt. *(Oakland Public Library)*

62

DIETZ OPERA HOUSE, OAKLAND.

Photographed during its heyday in the 1880s was Dietz Opera House, which stood at Twelfth and Webster Streets in Oakland. After the University of California deserted its Oakland campus, mansarded Brayton Hall, one of the buildings erected by Dr. Henry Durant, became an elegant social center for the burgeoning town. But in time a new opera house eclipsed it, and the old Dietz was reduced to accommodating prize fights and poultry shows. *(Albert Norman collection)*

the glory from the real hero, whose later arrival on his foam-flecked horse was a chaotic anticlimax. But, after all, celebrations were merely symbols, and the railroad, just as predicted, had given the whole East Bay a whopping shot in the arm.

The Pacific Tourist, a popular guide book published in New York by Crown, thus described Oakland of the mid-1870s: "Of all the suburbs of San Francisco, Oakland is the most popular. Its growth rate exceeds that of San Francisco. The time required to reach it from California Street is less than is required to get up-town from Wall Street in New York. It is beautiful for situation (with) scenery scarcely less picturesque than the banks of the Hudson affords. The rides in and around Oakland, for variety of attractive features, are rarely equalled. Many come over from San Francisco in the morning expressly to enjoy this

"It is a lovely sight to see A maiden in the privacy Of her own chamber ..." wrote an anonymous nineteenth century poet. This young East Bay matron of the 1870s sits embroidering surrounded by the sanctioned "internal decoration" of her day — fringed portieres, draped American flag, print of Christ praying at Gethsemane, marble busts and framed photographs.

pleasure. As measures of its enterprise and prosperity it may be stated that a quarter of a million dollars were expended in building a court-house and county jail. There are three savings banks, two national gold banks, five lines of horse-cars, three flouring and four planing mills, an iron and a brass foundry, two potteries, one patent marble works, a jute bag factory, three tanneries and other establishments employing many mechanics. Of the public schools . . . nearly a quarter of a million dollars value in property is owned by the department. There are 20 churches . . . some of them elegant and costly. Seven newspapers are published, two daily, the rest weekly. The population of the city increases rapidly, and is near 50,000."

Real estate speculation was in the air and refused to be dampened but slightly by the Panic of 1873. *Bishop's Oakland Directory* of 1878-1879 reported: "The attention of all who contemplated building near the Bay seemed directed to Oakland as a most promising field . . . there were 1,300

homes, large and small, erected here during America's Centennial Year of 1876." Property values were doubling roughly every two years.

Indeed, it was the correlation between the East Bay's galloping land values and its population increase that prompted young Henry George, who during the 1870s edited the Oakland *Transcript*, to formulate his famous economic theory. George held that land speculators, not ordinary citizens, were profiting from the "unearned increment" of land values inflated by heightened demand, and that a revision of the tax system to a "single tax" levy would prevent such profiteering. He said his theory first came to him while listening to a soap box speech in front of Oakland City Hall.

The East Bay was too busy expanding to ponder tax reform. "Merchant builders" devoted their energies to constructing speculative homes for sale, either for cash or on the installment plan. Among them was the corporate-owned Real Estate Union, organized in Oakland in 1874 with a

Pagoda Hill, an extravaganza of Byzantine and European influences was one of the sights of the East Bay when it stood on a rise overlooking Oakland's Chabot Road. It was the design of its owner, world-traveler J. Ross Browne, and heady mixture though it was, the composition contained both an original inventiveness and a certain harmony, which came of Browne's talent as an artist. His accomplished sketches served as illustrations for his numerous travel books and articles for HARPER'S WEEKLY.
(*Mrs. Spencer Browne collection*)

capital of nearly half a million dollars. In Alameda, the enterprising firm of Marcuse and Remmel built more than a hundred early homes. Some builders constructed homes for rental, for as low as $15 to $20 per month. And in every direction suburban tracts and subdivisions were being promoted by daring developers, among them Hall McAllister, brother of Ward McAllister, famed as "arbiter of New York's 400." Hall's sang-froid in real estate ventures was characterized by his once betting, and losing, in a poker game his handsome San Francisco mansion.

Real estate promotion had advanced in sophistication over the early land auctions drummed up with free bull fights and refreshments. The new foothills suburb of Piedmont was skillfully promoted by the Piedmont Land Company for its exclusiveness, but also as a "hillside health district," on the strength of a sulphur spring that bubbled near a resort hotel in a picturesque ravine called the "Bushy Dell" that was popular with courting couples. Minimized was Piedmont's abundance of coyotes, which prowled the early estate's lawns and gardens, and the acute shortage and costliness of water, which prompted even the rich to ration their children to two baths a week, often two to a tub.

One Charles Klinkner employed novel methods in publicizing the middle-income suburb of Klinknerville, located on the Bay between Oakland and Berkeley. On holidays he would paint a span of mules in holiday colors — green on St. Patrick's Day, red, white and blue on the Fourth of July, etc. — and drive them through Oakland hitched to a cart plastered with advertising; seated beside him in the cart were equally colorful dogs or monkeys. Over the street in front of his office, he stretched a huge banner blazoned: "KLINKNERVILLE REAL ESTATE. THIS IS THE PLACE. STOP HERE!" Klinkner's neighbors objected to the sign and had him arrested, but the judge, finding no statute in violation, ruled the sign legal.

The French mansard was but one of several architectural styles that were in favor during this building spree of the 1870s. Gothic continued popular for smaller houses, and the "aspiring design" also held its own among affluent builders. One late Gothic mansion of Christmas card beauty was an oblong design with three frothy front gables that Alfred C. Dietz built in north Oakland. Dietz, who had prospered in a San Francisco paint business, soon would convert one of the University's vacated Oakland buildings into Oakland's first opera house.

Byzantine influence was glimpsed here and there, especially in such details as arched doorways and rounded domes. Interest in the Near East had been kindled first by Bayard Taylor's popular travel book *The Land of the Saracen* and soon would get another boost from Dr. Richard Burton's shockingly erotic translation of *The Arabian Nights,* which Victorians bought like hot cakes on the grounds of erudition.

Pagoda Hill, the popular estate of the flamboyant confidential agent-ambassador-author J. Ross Browne, blended a strong measure of Byzantine with several other influences. An awed journalist, in 1875, wonderingly described the edifice situated on a twenty-acre exotically-landscaped hillside site in what is now Oakland's Claremont district, as: "A cupola from Moscow here, a Chinese gateway there, a Moorish dome on a French roof, a Saracenic belfry with a Japanese temple — all tossed together like the vagaries of a traveler's dream." Which was precisely what it was. Browne, who circled the globe several times in the course of duty to country and *Harper's Weekly,* upon returning from a stint as minister to China designed himself a house fashioned to remind him of each of his foreign assignments. Somehow, the visiting journalist managed to overlook the Italian, Gothic, and Indian features.

A warm-up for Pagoda Hill had been the rambling house that Browne built on the south rim of Lake Merritt in 1856. When he put it up for sale prior to going abroad, he described it as incorporating "the best of the Italian, Doric, Corinthian and Hindoo orders of architecture . . . the roof being Gothic . . ." Besides which, the house was almost completely embowered with the passion flower vine. Among many literary visitors to this house was Mark Twain, who admired Browne's wit and writing style. Once when jittery about an approaching lecture tour, Twain spent a week at the Brownes', practicing his anecdotes and gestures on the large Browne family. Bay Area literary gossip had it that Twain freely cribbed verbal yarns and quips from Browne, moreover used Browne's popular travel books as models for *Innocents Abroad.*

But in town and suburb, the most popular style for residences of less than mansion-size was Italianate. This design evolved from the discovery that the Italian villa's square, hooded tower looked foolish on a small house. The Italianate house was a sort of shrunken, solidified villa sans tower, but as though compensating for its loss, it wore a richer ornamentation.

By the early 1880s, Berkeley at long last had undergone incorporation. The Berkeley *Advocate* termed it a measure "which clothes the village of Berkeley with municipal honors and . . . a dignity commensurate with its importance." Yet, the south of campus district — note intersection of Durant and Ellsworth Streets — still retained a village look. Actually, Berkeley was experiencing a real estate boom, but it was concentrated mostly in West Berkeley, which was drawing both new residents and industries. *(Louis Stein collection)*

The Italianate house, also called the "bracketed style" because of the elaborate brackets under the eaves, provided a pleasant entry in the Victorian fashion parade. This one was the home of financier A. K. P. Harmon on Lake Merritt. He endowed the first Harmon Gymnasium at the University of California, an odd octagon-shaped cupolaed structure popularly known as the "ink bottle." *(Oakland Public Library)*

Replacing the villa's quiet detail — the simple arch, classic pediment, and light cornice — was a melange of rococo Italian features, mostly taken from the Seventeenth Century Mannerist period, which had been a reaction against the disciplines of the Renaissance. Windows now were elaborately dressed with segmented arches or square or broken pediments, these often set in double-tiered, angled bays and flanked with colonettes. Entrance porches rippled with fluted columns, turned balustrades, and decorated pediments, while cornice brackets grew so large and attention-calling as to give rise to the term "bracketed style." When overdone, these houses gave the impression of cluttered cubes, but they could also be executed with elegance, and they won those who had thought the villa a bit staid. This marriage of the formal and the picturesque seemed to express the sophisticated image that the busy, prospering Northern Californians had of themselves.

Just as the most rugged of men wept over sentimental Victorian novels, so did aggressive, masculine types house themselves in frilly Italianate. At the height of his world-wide fame as Alameda County's intrepid two-gun sheriff, Oakland's Harry Morse built himself an ornate Italianate house on which a fancy fretted portico balanced an equally furbeloved double bay. (His Nebraska idol, Buffalo Bill, soon afterward ensconced himself in an Italian villa.)

A New York City boy who had arrived at fourteen during the height of the gold rush, Morse, after a luckless try at the mines, went to work oaring boats and driving drays. He grew into a hulking, moon-faced, small-eyed six-footer with a takes-nothin'-offa-nobody reputation. He was setting himself up in the butcher business when

68

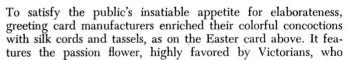

A peaceful happy Easter.

A Blithe New Year.

To satisfy the public's insatiable appetite for elaborateness, greeting card manufacturers enriched their colorful concoctions with silk cords and tassels, as on the Easter card above. It features the passion flower, highly favored by Victorians, who detected a resemblance in its botanical parts to certain symbols of the Crucifixion. The small cards at upper left are typical of the tokens of friendship left by gentlemen paying New Year's Day calls. Custom demanded that a young man leave a fancy card for each of the household's young ladies. At the end of the day, recipients totaled their colorful trophies and compared notes with their girl friends. Afterwards, the cards were pasted in "memory books."

(F. North collection)

TO GREET YOU ON EASTER DAY

Generations of Oaklanders visited this Italianate house at 1426 Lakeside Drive when it accommodated the Oakland Museum, below. Before that, it housed three prominent families: first the William Camerons, pictured left, with their domestic staff; the Josiah Stanfords (he was the governor's brother); and the John Wrights, who sold it to the city in 1907. When the house became a museum, its carriage house and ornamental chimneys were removed, but a rear extension was added for housing exhibits. Now vacant and forlorn, the house has been dubbed "The Old Lady of the Lake." (*Oakland* TRIBUNE.)

he was called upon to help defend Alameda County, then trembling with outlaw hysteria.

After providing a firm and cooling influence as Federal provost marshal, he was, at 28, elected sheriff with a mandate to get tough. He proved stern and terrible in the discharge of his duties. His eagerness to pursue his quarry into the hinterlands, his flash draw, and awesome aim gained him a reputation for "getting his man," among them the notorious Narrato Ponce, a killer reputed to be "superior in criminality" to the infamous Joaquin Murietta, and the elusive "Black Bart," who, before Harry Morse drew a bead on him, had gotten away with twenty-eight stage robberies.

In the end, Morse was defeated not by his adversaries, but by his fame. He couldn't mount his horse without being trailed by a vast posse of newsmen, including foreign correspondents, who kept the world and, of course, his quarry posted on his every maneuver. In 1874, thus encumbered and wearily frustrated but pressing doggedly on, Morse pursued a well-informed desperado almost to Los Angeles before giving up the trail. Soon after returning in disappointment to Oakland, he retired to his frothy palace with his ivory-handled six guns and his memories.

Other dynamic East Bay figures who chose the Italianate style for their residences were the brilliant Canadian-born hydraulic engineer Anthony Chabot, who built the water systems for San Francisco, Oakland, and other Bay Area cities; and Joseph Knowland of Alameda, whose grandson William, the former United States Senator, still directs the family publishing enterprise, the Oakland *Tribune*. A garlanded Italian palacio, replica of one on the Riviera, was the Alameda abode of Major Charles Lee Tilden, who installed the cable system for San Francisco's cable cars, operated a fleet of river boats, and founded the East Bay Regional Park System. Tilden Park was named after him. Today the well-kept palacio houses a doctor and his family. The Oakland sportsman Oscar Luning, son of railroad magnate Nicholas Luning, lived in an elegant Italianate mansion behind which were ranged the paddocks for his famous race horses, as well as Mrs. Luning's menagerie of imported goats, deer, coons, white rats, quail, and ring doves. The first residence on the University of California campus, the home of Professor Willard Rising was in the Italianate style, as was the home of Napoleon Bonaparte Byrne.

Two of the most tasteful Italian residences in the East Bay remain well-preserved today. One is the house John Alexander Anthony, a Southern Pacific Railroad official, built in 1876 on Alameda's Central Avenue and which stands today beside a giant magnolia. Its elegant facade has a most imposing entrance portico whose Mannerist pediment encloses a gracefully-incised entablature and is supported by slender fluted columns. Beautifully-moulded arched windows are accented with carved rosettes at their peaks. Behind the house is a large English natural garden which has been faithfully maintained in the height of the era's romantic taste; it is now shaded by overlapping aspen branches which admit a dim, subaqueous-like light upon the fern-bordered paths, one leading to a weathered sundial.

The other villa is the house on Lake Merritt and fronting on Oak Street that until 1968 housed the Oakland Museum and is probably the best-known residence in Oakland. For a few years after its construction, in 1876, it was the home of Alice Marsh, who was orphaned when her father Dr. John Marsh was ambushed in his buggy near Mount Diablo. Like her strange, ill-fated father, she too seemed star-crossed.

As a pretty Mills Seminary student, Alice fell in love with Will Cameron, a handsome cowboy. After she came into her sizable fortune, she and Will were married and they built the fashionable lake-side house, furnished it lavishly, and staffed it with servants. They were happy there for a time. Then their small daughter died suddenly of convulsions, after eating venison. A shadow fell over their lives; trying to erase the sad memory, they sold their home to Josiah Stanford, brother of Governor Leland Stanford. The Stanford home became the setting of a brilliant social life. President Rutherford B. Hayes was entertained there at a gala ball. But happiness eluded Alice. After a time she and Will were divorced; she never remarried.

The East Bay's two grandest residences of the Seventies were built in the waning Italian villa style. "The Highlands," Piedmont's first mansion, was built unstintingly with Comstock silver

Alameda not only was born Victorian but more than any other city in California has retained its Victorian atmosphere. This 1876 house at 1630 Central Avenue was built by railroad official John Anthony and is still owned by the same family. Its superb detailing, the arched windows, carved newel posts, and graceful portico, combine to make it a splendid example of the Italianate style. A committee of Alamedans is seeking to acquire it and maintain it as part of the permanent environment, such as another charming Italian style house, the former home of John Muir in Alhambra Valley, has been restored by the National Parks Service and designated a National Historic Site. The 1882 home of the famous writer-naturalist is now open to the public.

(Alameda TIMES STAR*)*

money, and was the answer to a developer's dream, for it dazzled and dominated and set the tone for future Piedmont construction more effectively than any ballyhoo could. It was a rectangular three-story house with classically-treated arched windows and doors with a square tower at one end and a gabled semi-tower at the other. It had twenty-two rooms, plus a harmonizing wing to house the large domestic staff and grounds crew. Crowning a commanding knoll high above Oakland and painted buttercup yellow with a chocolate brown trim, it was highly visible from San Francisco and more distant points. For decades it was the East Bay's most distinguishing landmark.

Dazzling too, in reputation, was The Highland's master, Isaac Requa, famed Comstock en-

gineer. Requa staked out some of the first claims on the site of the fabulous silver lode and was one of the leading figures in its development. He was superintendent of one of the three largest Virginia City mining companies, and also headed the engineering firm the companies hired jointly to drive 3150 feet below the earth to gain access to the hoped for extensions of the rich silver deposits. Later Requa served as president of the Central Pacific Railroad.

Requa's friends and associates were among the most prominent personalities of the era. While the other bonanza kings clustered on opulent Nob Hill, Requa preferred to cross the Bay and deploy over eighty rugged acres, there creating an almost self-sufficient establishment. The Highlands had its own illuminating gas plant, water supply, school house, athletic courts, cattle farm, orchards, vegetable gardens, and berry patches. There was even a doctor on the premises, this being Mrs. Requa, who during the years her husband prospected in remote mining camps before striking it rich, versed herself in the homeopathic school of medicine.

However, the Comstock hero cut himself off from neither society nor business. The elite of Oakland and San Francisco — the likes of C. P. Huntington, Senator James Fair of the Comstock's "Big Four," and A. K. P. Harmon — wound their way up the canyon road to dinners, balls, and financial confabs, up through the black and gold pillared gateway to the porte-cochere to be met by George Washington, the courtly mulatto butler. Carriages arrived too for Mrs. Requa's Wednesday at-homes and for children's parties for Mark and Amy Requa. Elaborate theatricals were staged for young guests from both sides of the Bay, among them Birdie and Tessie Fair, who, respectively, were to marry William K. Vanderbilt, Jr., and Herman Oelrichs and take their places as glittering hostesses of New York and Newport society.

Up the hill too rode top politicos, for though Requa repeatedly declined political office, he was a power behind the scenes in California politics.

Born in the mining camp of Chili Gulch, Major Charles Lee Tilden, after making a fortune in various transportation enterprises, ensconced himself in this palacio at 1031 San Antonio Avenue in Alameda. An example of Italianate at its most rococo, it was a copy of a San Francisco mansion that has since burned, which in turn had been copied from a palacio on the Italian Riviera. Breakfast and luncheon were served in the glassed-in porch that connected to the main dining room. In the Major's day, the house had extended grounds and included tennis and croquet courts, stable and horse paddock, cutting gardens, and conservatory. (Alameda TIMES STAR)

Fernside's more than seventy rooms made it the largest house in California, and when it was completed in Alameda in 1873, after fifteen months in construction, it was proclaimed the handsomest as well. It had four marble-columned entrances, tessellated marble floors, East Indian frescoes, and a ballroom with floor-to-ceiling mirrors. Its master was transportation expert A. A. Cohen and its designer the architecture firm of Wright and Saunders of San Francisco. After it was completed, Mark Hopkins asked them to design his Nob Hill mansion. The center of lavish entertainment, Fernside dazzled and dominated the East Bay social scene until it burned at the turn of the century.

Above and at right are views of the spacious third-floor hall and of the commodious carriage house, the latter a stereopticon view by the famous photographer Edward Muybridge. Fernside was furnished by the prestige New York furniture houses of Sloan's and Herter's. Much of the furniture was of the Egyptian-inspired motif that was highly fashionable in the early 1870s. (*Mrs. Augustin C. Keane collection*)

His son Mark inherited his political bent and was highly influential as Republican National Committeeman; he served too as advisor to President Calvin Coolidge and, later, masterminded the presidential nomination of his friend and fellow engineer Herbert Hoover.

However, the most splendid of all Italian villas in the East Bay was "Fernside," the Alameda home of the brilliant attorney and transportation expert Alfred A. Cohen. Fernside was grandly situated amidst fifty lush acres of gardens and orchards — Cohen was also a horticultural expert. The mansion was said to have been modeled after the summer home of Queen Victoria, whose subject Cohen was as a youth. The vast towered three-story, rectangular structure enclosed more than seventy rooms. With its sweeping carriage entrance and double porte-cochere, it rather resembled a luxury hotel at a fashionable spa.

Interior features most noted by journalists were its East Indian frescoes and a twenty-five-foot-wide entrance hall whose grand staircase was illuminated by a magnificent domed skylight. Two of the Central Pacific Railroad's "Big Four," Leland Stanford and Charles Crocker, with whom Cohen was associated, came to inspect Fernside when it was building and later incorporated some of its features into their own palaces.

They may have come later to inspect the Cohen library and art gallery, for the erudition and art connoisseurship in which they then were tutoring themselves came naturally to the many-faceted Cohen. His gallery, which occupied an entire floor, was sought out by the painter Albert Bierstadt when he visited California, and Bierstadt later presented Cohen one of his own works to hang there. Cohen was among the first to recognize the talent of the young San Francisco portraitist Charles Nahl and commissioned him to paint the Cohen children.

His library of more than 50,000 volumes was singled out for comment in the book *The Libraries of California*, published in 1878, which called it "probably the choicest private collection of books in the state." That commendation doubtless helped underscore the latest gossip on one of the other railroad kings: that he was ordering books by the yard to fill his elegant new bookcases.

The handsome, fastidious son of a London aristocrat, Cohen had been lured by gold rush excitement from his family's business operations in Jamaica. Upon arriving in California, he set himself up as a commission merchant in Sacramento and profited quickly. Marrying the daughter of a San Francisco doctor, he stayed on in California after the gold rush and made a fortune transporting people about the mushrooming Bay Area via narrow-gauge railroads and ferryboats. After the transcontinental railroad was completed and looked like a poor money-maker, the Big Four tapped Cohen to serve as their advisor, which he did, much to the railroad's profit and his own.

While working closely with the Big Four, Cohen always considered himself culturally a cut above those small-town merchants who had hit the big time. He once complained that his job had compelled him to associate with "men whose manner, whose habits, whose modes of thought and conversation were not calculated to advance me." He publicly credited Stanford with "the ambition of an emperor and the spite of a peanut vendor." But he reserved his consummate disdain for the 250-pound Crocker who had found his calling driving Chinese railroad gangs across the Sierra but who in later life aspired to the culturati and embarked on a much-publicized trip to Europe to collect art. Cohen was singularly unimpressed with the resulting assemblage. He characterized Crocker as a "waddling monument to the triumph of vulgarity," and told it of him that he had set out intending "to employ Mr. Medici himself to make the selections" and had purchased Gobelin tapestries and then employed someone to tell him "whether they should be hung upon the walls as paintings or spread upon the floor." Naturally, Cohen's victims smoldered under his rapier wit — though not enough to deprive themselves of his acumen. Nor did Cohen's offended sensibilities persuade him to relinquish the lucrative association. He was on company business when he died, in 1887, on a railway train.

With his superior tone and aesthetic finicking, Cohen, while a cultural pace setter, was quite attuned to the East Bay's wave length. While San Franciscans reveled in their so-called "champagne days," their eastward neighbors prided themselves on quaffing things of the spirit. They were given to boasting, "We cater to the inner man, San Francisco to the innard."

These self-styled Brahmins hurled themselves passionately into cultural pursuits of all descriptions: into the Chickering Club, whose members read their own poetry and prose compositions and recited the classics; into choral groups with as many as 700 voices, into harmonic societies, piano ensemble groups, instrumental clubs, orchestras, amateur operas and theatricals; into lyceum series, at which one staple was the scholarly travel lecture (which may account for some of the popular given names of the period — India, Armenia, Vienna, Persia, Paris, etc.) In the 1870s, both Oakland and Alameda opened public libraries (Dr. Merritt helped found Oakland's), which promptly acquired waiting lists for books on self-improvement and moral uplift. Oakland's first librarian was Ina Coolbrith, who would become California's first Poet Laureate. Housewives, ministers, merchants, and schoolgirls had their leather-bound pocket volumes of poetry to dip into as inspiration-chargers. Oakland women made history by organizing the state's first women's club, the Ebell Society, christened after an Eastern scholar and subsumed into myriad "study sections." Contemplating this rich fare, the Oakland *Enquirer* rhapsodized, "Oakland is populated by lotus eaters!"

East Bay erudition was highly, if indirectly, complimented by an editorial in the Oakland *Daily News,* which complained that its subscribers were so discriminating they were intimidating its staff: "Here lie a people cultivated, aristocratic and hard to please, and the local journalist who can come up to their requirements must be a man of liberal education, originality of thought, and with some felicity of expression. And so, one after another has come and gone . . . horribly disgusted with 'Oakland's unappreciative inhabitants.'" Later this captiousness was noted in a sign that hung backstage at New York's Palace Theater: "If you think your act is good, play Oakland."

The East Bay's self-esteem can't be dismissed merely as local chauvinism; the locality's high intellectual tone was concurred in by disinterested observers. Charles Lorin Brace in his book *The New West,* published in the 1870s, expressed en-

thusiasm for Oakland, which he reported to be "drawing to itself all the best educational institutions and the most intelligent society of the state . . . this is undoubtedly to be the intellectual center of the whole region west of the Sierra." One high tribute came from a prominent San Franciscan, Mrs. Flora Haines Apponifi, who stated in a magazine article: "Although only four or five miles of salt water separates the suburban town of Oakland from the parent city, a curious difference in the social structure of the two places is evident. . . . The coarser element of urban life remains at home. People of vulgar tastes and loud ambitions find the best opportunity for their exercise in a larger city. The people who have taken their abode across the bay are essentially refined."

But while revering rarified culture, the East Bay by no means forsook society's fads and fashions. Hostesses were *au courant* in the latest Eastern modes in entertainment and decor. When the Kirkham mansion on Lake Merritt was *en fête* for the wedding of Major Kirkham's daughter, Lelia, to the Englishman who later became a lord and made her Lady Yard-Buller, California was introduced to an Eastern custom then brand new. Late arrivals found the veranda teeming with guests, many from San Francisco, complaining, "It's so dark inside you can't see your hand before you." The crowd was finally coaxed indoors, where the wedding took place in dim gaslight in rooms from which all sunlight had been excluded. The puzzled guests became more respectful of the shadowy tableau when they read in the society columns that they had witnessed the latest thing in New York high society—daytime entertaining in darkened rooms.

And no sooner had the "Japanese mania" gripped the Eastern Seaboard, inspired by the Japanese exhibit at the Philadelphia Centennial of 1876, than it popped up in the East Bay. Interiors suddenly blossomed out with gayly-colored Japanese fans and parasols, the fans grouped wide open and tacked on walls in half or full circles, while parasols were opened and laid on edge in corners. The husband who wonderingly inquired, "Why leave an open umbrella in the corner?" was squelched with, "Because it's *artistic.*" "Artistic" was the important new word in the decorator's lexicon. Another term for such studied effects —

draping an Oriental shawl over a piano or pedestal was also popular — was "giving a room a studio touch."

However, while propriety and fashion were deferred to, anything smacking of ostentation was frowned upon. The typical East Bay homemaker subscribed to the Victorian dictum that the home arts were to be directed neither toward display nor sensual enjoyment, but toward moral uplift. As one home expert put it, the house "refines and purifies the hearts of her household by surrounding them with things of beauty." Beauty and harmony, it was believed, made one good. Of course, every true Victorian harbored the urge to flaunt his possessions as proof of material success. For *no* Victorian low-rated material success; after all, material things as a reward for virtue was a staple of Victorian novels and sermons. Every hostess struggled between these two opposing tugs, but in the East Bay it was the former that pulled most forcibly, as in San Francisco the latter usually exerted the stronger magnetic field.

It was a leg up socially for former saloon-keeper James Flood when he encircled his Nob Hill mansion with a $30,000 bronze fence and hired a full-time polisher to keep it shining like some gargantuan glowworm. Some Nob Hill butlers were decked out in velvet uniforms with buttons the size of pocket watches. East Bay extravagances took more discreet forms, for example, the exact replica of Cardinal Thomas Wolsey's Gothic dining room at Hampton Court that hardware tycoon Peter White installed, in 1876, in his Alameda mansion, thus combining splendor with scholarship. Likewise, the costly conservatories and aviaries, while titillating the senses, were revered as educational.

This East Bay moralizing and circumspection were guides in selecting architectural style during the mid-Victorian era. One selected a style — or thought he did — not for its prettiness, but for its intrinsic character. Gothic was inspiring, Italian was dignified, French was dynamic, like Napoleon. A formal house plan of square, straight-ranged rooms was thought to encourage an orderly existence, whereas an irregular plan would inject a sense of freedom into one's life. And opinion dictated that whatever style one selected it should be executed with a restrained hand that eschewed bold bids for attention, such as marked some of San Francisco's sham castles, wedding cake houses, and angry castellations.

Caution sometimes made for a certain monotony; East Bay houses of the mid-Victorian era on the whole were more to be admired collectively, than individually. Substantial and conformingly stylish, alas, they were somewhat standardized. To be sure, the East Bay was not without its *nouveaux riches* in whose breasts palpitated the urge to tell the world they had risen, and tell it in the most direct way with a flamboyant abode. But community tone sternly discouraged the impulse. Even Frederick "Bottleneck" Koenig, who operated a scarcely muted Barbary Coast establishment, when in residence in Oakland looked out at the world from the classically pedimented windows of his mansarded mansion.

It goes without saying that all this disciplined restraint, this scrupulous underplaying of material success in the interests of character-building, was not lacking in purpose — nothing Victorian ever was. And what was that purpose, exactly? Why, more success, of course!

"The Cedars," near left, was built by Napoleon Bonaparte Byrne. He bought 827 acres in north Berkeley, built this Italianate house at 1300 Oxford Street and planted many of the cedars, pines, oak, and cypress that survive today in Live Oak Park. After losing his fortune in an ambitious farming scheme, Byrne lived in this modest 1880 Italianate house, far left, next door to his former mansion. (*Louis Stein collection*)

The drawing room at Arbor Villa exemplifies the height of Victorian elegance. Femininity reigns supreme in its ceiling fresco paintings, French furniture, and the "Golden Tapestry" depicting the marriage of Queen Esther. While the popularity of French furniture waned in the 1880s, its delicacy and grace were still preferred for the really sumptuous setting, especially for drawing rooms. A recent development in furniture-making was the creation of "sets" of matched furniture. Here two similar sets of French furniture are mingled in the two adjoining sitting areas. *(Oakland Public Library)*

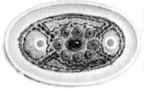

$uch an $ltitude of $iving !

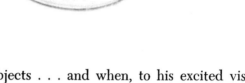

In 1907, during a much-heralded round-the-world cruise on his yacht "The Snark," with success dazzling round him like a halo and his pretty second wife Charmian spelling him at the tiller, Jack London, who had scored with accounts of exotic places and adventures, wrote a novel set in Oakland. *Martin Eden* was its title, and its time setting was the late Victorian Era. That was when London was growing up as a deck hand on the roisterous Oakland water front, and intimates say the novel chronicled London's own experience. If so, then the most formative event in his life, as it was for the novel's highly-impressionable protagonist, was being invited to one of Oakland's fashionable mansions.

The fictional young sailor Martin Eden received the fateful invitation as a reward. While ferrying to Oakland from San Francisco, he rescued the scion of the prominent Morse family from the clutches of a gang of roughnecks and got invited home to dinner.

Upon arriving at the entrance hall of the august Morse mansion, Martin was gripped with panic and tried to stuff his grimy cap into his pocket. The parlor with its grand piano, centre table arranged with books, and oil paintings of waves pounding rocks so awed Martin that he swayed upon his feet and was "in terror lest his shoulders should collide with the doorways or sweep the bric-a-brac from the low mantel . . . He recoiled from side to side between the various objects . . . and when, to his excited vision, one arm seemed liable to brush against the books on the table, he lurched away like a frightened horse, barely missing the piano stool."

At this nadir of Martin's discomfiture, his host introduced him to his sister, "a pale ethereal creature with wide, spiritual blue eyes," whom Martin learned to his tongue-tied consternation, was an English major at the University of California at Berkeley. Marshalling himself to a show of *sang-froid*, he boasted that he had read "Excelsior" and the "Psalm of Life" and hazarded a comment on the volume of Swinburne on the centre table, pronouncing it "*Swine*burne." For which Miss Morse promptly corrected him. "Here was intellectual life," he thought in a daze of admiration, but in it he felt "like a navigator adrift on a strange sea without chart or compass."

Dinner was an even more grueling ordeal with its baffling array of silverware and dainty cut glass. Never had he seen "such an altitude of living." It seemed to him that "he had never worked so hard in his life . . . Tiny nodules of moisture stood out on his forehead, and his shirt was wet with sweat from the exertion of doing so many unaccustomed things at once." Here he was sitting "shoulder to shoulder, at dinner, with people he had read about in books." Whenever one of the splendid assembly addressed him as "Mr. Eden," it transported him into ecstasy, but then he would be cast to the depths again by a

79

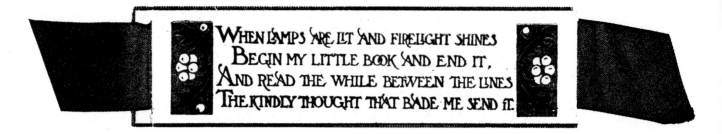

When lamps are lit and firelight shines
Begin my little book and end it,
And read the while between the lines
The kindly thought that bade me send it.

This bookmark of paper and ribbon with holly motif was
designed to accompany a gift book. *(North collection)*

wondering stare at his rough, red hands, and he would know he was out of it, "not of their tribe."

After dinner Miss Morse played selections on the grand piano, and to Martin her playing seemed one more reproach, as if the music "was a club that she swung brutally upon his head." Yet, at the same time, her music stimulated him to "audacities of feeling." When the time came for him to beat a stumbling retreat, the ethereal English major lent him the volume of Swinburne and another of Browning. Thereupon, Martin "pulled on his cap, lurched desperately through the doorway, and was gone." It had been the most galvanizing experience of his life.

One exposure to that grand house convinced Martin that he must lift himself out of society's cellar and into the realm of the Morses. But how to ascend to those rarefied heights? Martin didn't know. He only knew that he must return to that house, and he realized with joy that he had a pretext: to return the books!

Alas, he hadn't the faintest notion how soon he might properly return them, nor what time of day to call. He hastened to the Oakland Free Library to consult an etiquette book on this point, also on how to disport himself in such a house. (He probably consulted the trusted *Hill's Manual*, which instructed with sketches of louts insulting genteel parlors by wearing hats, standing with arms akimbo, sitting astride chairs, etc.) Martin spent hours in the library thus grooming himself for his return, and when at home he brushed his teeth, scrubbed his hands with a brush, took baths, and pressed creases in his clothes.

Martin's return was a success. This time, with his handy frame of reference he got on easily. Miss Morse made him feel so comfortable that he was moved to confide: "I want to breathe air like you get in this house — air that is filled with books, and pictures, and beautiful things. . . . I want to make my way to the kind of life you have in this house. . . . Now, how am I goin' to get it?" Miss Morse gently told him that he would need an education, and since he hadn't any he would need to start from scratch. "I should say the first thing would be to get a grammar. Your grammar is . . ." She had intended saying "awful," but amended it to, "is not particularly good." Martin blushed at this but was not downcast, especially after Miss Morse offered to assist him with his studies at regular afternoon sessions in the Morse parlor. This time when Martin departed the grand house, he carried with him not merely a yearning to scale the heights, but a modus operandi: he would acquire an education the way he acquired the manners of a gentleman by siphoning up the book-bound knowledge in the Oakland Free Library. And in the course of the novel Martin does.

One can readily see how one of Oakland's grand late Victorian mansions, the splendid facade, glittering furnishings, and polished inhabitants might have so overwhelmed a poor "wharf rat" as to change his life. Of course, Victorian design never tended to understatement, but during the 1880s and early 1890s it reached a zenith of expression. Never before nor since abounded such a wide selection of residential styles, nor styles so richly ornamented. It was at this time that the notion that enrichment could never be overdone reached the furthermost swing of the pendulum, the point from which began the rebound swing to the Twentieth Century conviction succinctly summed up by Bauhaus-trained architect Mies van der Rohe as "Less is more."

Also never before had architects engaged in such unabashed style mixing. The most esteemed

The mansard had a late echo in the exuberant Stick Villa style — sometimes called Barbary Coast Gothic. The style combined a pointed tower or semi-tower with the use of exterior framing strips, especially at corners and windows, these applied over horizontal siding. Some Stick Villas contained an admixture of Eastlake details, as does famed Carson House in Eureka. Above is the Knowles residence at Fifteenth and Jackson Streets and, right, the home of I. W. Tabor on Madison Street. (*Albert Norman collection*)

architect was the one who could manipulate the most motifs, while adding his own hybrid to the pleasure garden. For the late Victorian, variety was the spice of life, the more so when all possible varieties were enjoyed at once. The Oakland *Tribune* complimented this heady potpourri in its issue of January 3, 1891: "Architecturally, Oakland has improved wonderfully of late. The great variety introduced by the architects and adopted by the builders is surprising. Every classic, medieval and Eastern style is blended (and is) mixed with the fancies and whims of the designer and those for whom he designs. The consequence is that a marvelous yet pleasing variety and contrast are shown throughout the city, from palatial mansion to modest cottage."

Likewise beaming approval was the influential *Artistic Homes of California,* an elaborate album of photo engravings published in San Francisco in 1888 for parlor enjoyment. The editor devoted generous attention to East Bay residences, noting that designs were "no mere repetition of each other"; and that, in fact, some houses could not be classified at all inasmuch as they "combined all the different orders."

Seemingly, there wasn't a shrinking violet among them, and yet this full cornucopia of richness and variety was not really so contentious as today's reader might suppose. These late Victorian styles, different as they were, scrambled though they might be, had as common denominators the qualities of virility, boldness, sentiment, and, above all, ornateness. One in spirit, they enjoyed a merry coexistence.

Richness and variety was scarcely confined to architecture. Interior decoration — then called "internal decoration" — was just as eclectic. It guilelessly assembled, under one roof, styles from several periods of European furnishings, borrowings from the Near East and the Orient, while blending in an exciting, brand new entry called Eastlake, which had just wafted in from Queen Victoria's England. Juxtaposition was the least of problems. A statuette of a harem odalisque might genially share the same spotlight with a curious, glass-dome-covered object concocted of the hair of a dear, departed aunt.

So insatiable was the appetite for variety in the Bay Area that local architects borrowed the motif of that new English furniture and converted

An 1888 photograph of Oakland's Alice Street displays the rampant eclecticism of the decade. Here coexisting, either individually or in combination, are Mansard, Stick, Gothic, Eastlake, and Queen Anne styles. (*Albert Norman collection*)

This was the childhood home of the famous Julia Morgan who left a towering mark on American architectural history. The Charles Morgan home, before which she posed with a younger brother, is a blend of Stick-Eastlake and Queen Anne, both English-derived motifs. Her chief inspiration would prove to be the styles from the sunny Mediterranean. When she left for Paris after graduating from the University of California, her departure was thus noted in the Oakland weekly *Saturday Night:* "Miss Morgan will sail for Europe, where she will study in Paris for a year under skillful masters. Oakland will be very proud in the future of her woman architect — for Miss Julia Morgan has rare ability, a capacity for work, and is with it all very popular among a large circle of friends." (*North collection*)

83

This substantial Stick-style house, which stood at 2001 East Twenty-eighth Street in the leafy Highland Park district, was the home of George R. Babcock, who had a long career in Oakland city administration. The wall sur- face cover includes pearl-cut shingles, plain shingles, and horizontal boarding, while the mullioned windows feature a variety of art nouveau glass. *(Albert Norman collection)*

it into a distinct residential style that became California's first architectural export. Eastlake furniture, which had made its American debut at the Philadelphia Centennial of 1876, was the brainchild of Londoner Charles Eastlake who was seeking to woo the public away from curvaceous French influences into "sincere" interiors. His furniture was straight, squared-off and flat-surfaced, but correctly surmising that Victorians were unready to abandon ornament, he embellished his rectilinear planes with incised designs, variously floral or geometric. Decorators, who sensed that anything so revolutionary would be good for business, seized upon Eastlake, claiming that to substitute it for sensual cabriole legs and curving arms would have a salubrious effect upon character, especially male natures. One decorator averred that "the soothing influence of an Eastlake bookcase on an irritated husband has never been sufficiently calculated."

But it remained for Bay Area architects to channel those influences into architectural design. They made the discovery that Eastlake's floral and geometric designs looked handsome applied to the new angular "Stick" architectural style which had gravitated to the Coast from the Midwest. In Stick construction support framing was applied on exteriors in stylized patterns. Strips crisply flanked windows and doors and reinforced corners, square bays and eaves; crisscrossed strips oftentimes were laid on the planes, rather in the manner of Elizabethan half-timbering.

At first, Eastlake designs were confined to the framing sticks. But the English foliation so thrived under the Western sun that it soon was creeping over exteriors like a tropical vine. Lathe-cut patterns undulated anywhere and everywhere. The better to give the design free play, verandas were dispensed with and entrances relegated to one side. The facade became, in effect, a huge wood mosaic, at the center of which, the focus of the eye, was a dazzling decorative panel, which the home owner often was given the privilege of selecting. The panel might be hand-carved, or ordered ready-made from a planing mill. Sometimes Eastlake designs were moulded into terra cotta insets. In tasteful hands, these exteriors were as stunning as a Byzantine altarpiece, which they in some ways resembled; in inept ones, they suggested a crazy quilt, as press detractors were quick to observe.

Some photographs of the latter came to the attention of Mr. Eastlake who found them hardly "sincere." From London came his less than delighted response: "I now find, to my amazement, that there exists on the other side of the Atlantic an 'Eastlake style' of architecture, which judging from the (California) specimens I have seen illustrated, may be said to burlesque such doctrines of art as I have ventured to maintain."

Mr. Eastlake's cool breath withered the California exuberance not at all. Stick-Eastlake facades proliferated like dandelions on both sides of the Bay, adorning both mansions and cottages alike. For the latter, the San Francisco *Bulletin* published a how-to-do-it plan with specifications covering everything from labor to screws and including a picket fence, so exactly computed that the cost toted up to exactly $3388.22. Further, the airy crisp design won converts across the country after it received a rave review in *American Architect*. For the first time an architectural fashion spread from California eastward, instead of the other way around.

Some of the East Bay's most ambitious homes of the 1880s and early 1890s were Stick-Eastlakes. Ely W. Playter, banker and hardware merchant who was Oakland's mayor in the mid-eighties, lived sumptuously in a three-story Stick-Eastlake mansion; it later lifted the spirits of working girls after it became the East Bay's first residential YWCA. The rich Eastlake exterior of the John

M. Buffington home was heightened by a parti-colored paint scheme, thus described in *Artistic Homes of California*: "The basement portion is dark green; above that is a band of dark terra-cotta, which is repeated in the window-casings. The first story is dark red, then a band of olive. Above that, in fancy shingles, is the second story in light green. The gables are ornamented with disks of contrasting colors."

But that wasn't all. Often the effect was crowned with a pitched shingled roof of contrasting colors, or a crested mansard. Square towers were added to the scheme, these frequently mansarded, and it was this last addition that prompted one critic to protest that the situation had reached a point of "architectural hysteria."

Still, this ultimate variety, also called Stick Villa and Barbary Coast Gothic, could win and hold admirers, as demonstrated by famed Carson House in Eureka, probably the most popular Victorian house in America and a set for numerous movies. Carson House was designed by the Newsome brothers architecture firm of San Francisco, which also designed the home of Oakland hardware merchant Wallace Everson, a near replica, except that its tower was lower and its roof was accented with a forest of finials as elaborate as royal scepters. *Artistic Homes of California* called this residence of one of the charter directors of the exclusive Athenian Club "one of the most attractive houses in Oakland."

One of the East Bay's most fanciful Stick-Eastlakes was the towered Alameda residence of Joseph Forderer, the talented maker of cornices for many of Northern California's public buildings during his time (Lick Observatory, Pacific Union Club, Napa State Hospital). Forderer, who was also an Alameda city official, lived in a fantastic house that for some suggested a Victorian valentine, to others an enchanted cottage in the Black Forest. It was an Alameda landmark until its demolition a decade ago.

Even more arresting than the Forderer house is the facade of the so-called King Estate, which still diverts passers-by on Oakland's Sixth Avenue. This former abode of timber tycoon Charles H. King for whom King City was named combines almost equal parts of Stick-Eastlake and Italian-

A bemused suitor might have had difficulty deciding which entrance of the King Estate to ascend, not to speak of which balcony to serenade under. The architect of this thirty-eight-room mansion at 1043 Sixth Avenue in Oakland also seems to have been undecided, hesitating between the Italianate and Eastlake styles, although the latter did get the upper hand. Once it was the mansion of lumber baron Charles H. King, for whom King City was named, and if a curio today, in its heyday it was an important social center. Its drawing room and ballroom, each seventy feet long, vibrated with the splendid social affairs of the large, dynamic King family. Especially dazzling was the daughter Pearl, who according to an Oakland society column excelled in both "literary studies" and the "correct interpretation of elocution work," moreover, "could be a fine concert pianist, but of course she doesn't have to do it, and so her wonderful talent developed with rare perseverance is for her home and friends." Pearl, who was also beautiful, made her social debut in the brilliantly lighted King drawing room before five hundred California elite, who were treated to dancing to a string orchestra and a multi-course dinner. The debutante was described as dressed in an "exceedingly artistic" mousseline de soie Paris gown and "with the quaint curl over one shoulder, she looked as if she might have stepped out of some exquisite picture." Having made her social bows, Miss King decided to take one of her talents out of the realm of home and friends. She went to New York and there behind the gas jet footlights blossomed into the versatile actress Pearl Tanner.

87

ate. The 38-room structure was not one facade, but a rippling succession of ornate fronts, which recede both in height and in depth — possibly why it is called an estate instead of a house. The whole rather suggests a house that possessed the ability of reproducing itself by multiplying, while lacking the ability to divide.

Each facade is liberally endowed with decorative Eastlake strips, floral inset panels, and a pediment, variously placed over windows and the entrance porch, that features a half sunburst design, a popular Eastlake motif. Italianate is represented by arched windows, colonnettes, and ornate cornice brackets. Being in lumber, King may have wished his house to demonstrate the limitless intricacy that lumber permitted. The house has a theatrical quality, and one of King's daughters who grew up in it, after making her social debut before five hundred of the Bay Area elite, went to New York and became an actress under the name of Pearl Tanner. Later, she was a top star in early radio.

While less spectacular for lack of scope, cottage-sized Stick-Eastlakes could put up a bold front. Some utilized an abundance of scroll cut; on some incised strips were applied as board-and-batten, or were crisscrossed, Elizabethan style. Herbert Hoover, in 1896, fresh out of Stanford, lived in a modest but frilly Stick-Eastlake on Oakland's Twelfth Street. Fancy shingles and a spindled arch added to its lacy effect. Hoover, then starting his career as a $35-a-month office boy for a firm of mining engineers, shared the residence with his orphaned brother and sister.

While mansion-sized Stick-Eastlakes are fast disappearing, numerous of these smaller versions abound in the East Bay. Most of their facades have been muted by time and a practice of painting them in a single pastel shade, instead of in contrasting Victorian colors. On Lafayette Street in Alameda stand two delightful Stick-Eastlake cottages, both constructed by the same contractor, in 1894. Today both are painted green, yet each has its distinct personality. One has for a centerpiece a sunburst design the size of a wagon wheel, this set against a spiky geometric backdrop. The cynosure of the other is a Japanese fan, opened against a lacy background in which floral figures and tendrils predominate; this house is slightly smaller and of a softer green. The pair rather suggest an Oriental potentate and his queen, grown old together.

One wonders whose personality those gay centerpieces expressed. Doubtless the qualms the modern woman suffers when choosing textiles for the living room is nothing compared to the strain of selecting those Eastlake centerpieces. A woman in the throes of selection must have felt she was mounting herself on a billboard for all the world to judge. And indeed a century later some are still being judged.

One other American-bred style, although not California-bred, sparked a flurry in the East Bay. This was Richardson Romanesque, which came about because an American architecture student at the École des Beaux-Arts went traveling in the South of France and became enamored of the old Romanesque churches built during the Crusades. These old churches were of a vaguely Roman style, or what was dimly remembered of it through the Dark Ages — chunky stone piles with bulky ornament, big semi-circular arches, short, fat columns, and round, blunt towers. Henry Hobson Richardson, an exceedingly talented young man, saw that with modifications the style could be adapted to the needs of modern residences and public buildings.

Back at his drawing board in Boston, he largely dispensed with the bulky representational ornament, retaining the rough-hewn stone, large detailing and massive piers. What he came up with was quite a new look in architecture, one that contrasted sharply with the prevailing Victorian minutiae. The wide arches served him not only for entrances, but as great frames for containing rows of small-paned windows. Bulky towers, some round, some square, were wrapped around corners, accommodating large rooms. Richardson further undertook a new idea in architecture, that of letting the purpose of a building determine its form. His undulating designs were highly pleasing, rather suggesting his own fastidious rotundity. Eastern millionaires found this legacy from Crusades' piety just the thing for expressing, both in their mansions and their factories, their chosen images of monumentality and strength.

Romanesque was several years late in reaching the West Coast, and once arrived it first found

Richardson Romanesque, inspired by the French ecclesiastical architecture of the Crusades era, arrived in California belatedly, and then hit a snag on domestic architecture. Whereas earlier Victorian styles had translated readily into wood construction, this fortress-like motif resisted. Most Romanesque frame houses looked dumpy and stolid. However, certain Romanesque features, such as its wide arch and rounded corner tower, blended harmoniously with other styles. In the Kimball house on Jackson Street, Romanesque complemented Queen Anne. *(Albert Norman collection)*

Romanesque was more purely used in California public and commercial architecture. The first Stiles Hall, the University YMCA, was built in the Romanesque mode in 1892, situated opposite the Dana Street entrance to the University campus. Long used as a campus lecture and concert hall, it was demolished in the late 1920s to make way for the present Harmon Gymnasium. *(Berkeley Firefighters Association)*

more admirers than adherents. Whereas Italian villas and mansards had translated pliantly into wood, the bulging designs intended for rusticated stone resisted. Public building projects, which permitted masonry construction, were more receptive to Romanesque. But even in these structures, stone was rarely the prime material; more frequently brick was used with stone trim, often the dark-blue sandstone quarried in Niles Canyon. Brick was also combined with the new moulded terra cotta that was becoming popular.

Richardson's Trinity Church, built for the pulpit of the esteemed Boston preacher, Phillips Brooks, was then probably the most popular building in America, so Romanesque was a natural for churches. In 1890, Oakland's First Unitarian congregation built a handsome Romanesque church of red brick and white stone with square bell tower and arched side entrance, the design of architect W. J. Matthew. The Oakland *Tribune* called it "the most notable structure in the city." The First Church of Christ Scientist built a Romanesque church of a rather similar design, also in brick and stone. Oakland Roman Catholics built their Sacred Heart church in traditional Romanesque, all in carven rusticated stone. All three churches are still in use.

Romanesque stamped one city hall in the East Bay. Alameda built its impressive city hall in red brick with white stone to accent its wide arches and square clock tower. When dedicated in 1896 with festive ceremonies, whose program was printed in the shape of the new building, its reception was so enthusiastic plans were made to build a whole civic center in Romanesque, but this was never carried through. The building no longer has its tower, which was toppled by the earthquake.

New Romanesque buildings went up in business districts all over the East Bay, among them Oakland's still impressive Central Building on Broadway, built of brick with terra cotta trim and ornamentation. Smaller commercial buildings in Berkeley, on Alameda's High Street, and on Oakland's San Pablo Avenue utilized the light-giving big Romanesque arch with insets of multiple-paned windows.

The *Architectural Record* had warned that "none but a lunatic" would undertake to construct a Romanesque building in wood. But a population so avid for novelty as the Bay Area could not pass up the temptation to Romanesque their houses, and inevitably in the expanding East Bay suburbs appeared a style called "Modern Romanesque." The design was a dumpy shingle house, one front corner of which was moulded into a gargantuan octagonal semi-tower; in front center stood a stolid columned portico. This lump of dead weight rested on a plain elevation of blue sandstone. Translation had been carried one step too far; the house looked neither modern or Romanesque, and the best one hedging writer would say for it was that the style was "very new" and "one of Oakland's latest designs." Its vogue was of short duration.

More successfully, Romanesque was tossed into the rich California mix, where there was always room for more. Bits and pieces of Romanesque began to appear on new residences. The big square towers with ranges of long narrow win-

In the Romanesque style was Mary Stuart Hall at the California Baptist College, built on a rise in the new subdivision of Highland Park. The suburb was developed in the early 1880s by E. C. Sessions, who bordered each block with eucalyptus and cypress trees, giving a park-like appearance. Many well-known families lived in the pleasant neighborhood, which later became the site of Highland Hospital. (*Albert Norman collection*)

Dedicated with festive ceremony in 1896 was the new Alameda City Hall, built in the Richardson Romanesque style at a cost of $56,884. The design was reminiscent of many railroad stations built throughout the West and Midwest. The elaborate tasseled dedication program in the shape of the new building boasted that Alameda was the healthiest city of the Pacific Coast, had a perfect sewer system, and was "rapidly becoming the most beautiful suburban residence city in America." (*Alameda Free Library*)

dows, such as those that dominated some of Richardson's railroad stations, were wedded to houses of a variety of styles.

Possibly the most handsome Romanesque blend in the East Bay was the one Joseph C. Newsome, of the Newsome brothers' architecture office, designed for himself in the new suburb of Linda Vista Terrace on Oakland's northern fringe. With every style at his fingertips, Newsome chose to combine Romanesque with what he termed "modernized Colonial." Possibly weary of serving up frills and furbelows, he made his architectural statement so simple and clean-cut as to appear almost Twentieth Century. His plain high roof was cut by a row of very attenuated, needle-like dormers, while the shingled house rounded out on one side into a very fat, blunt semi-tower. The great arched entrance in front-center was left untreated by anything but an extension of the shingles which bulged and curved as though moulded.

The house, painted a dark yellow with roof of silver gray, must have stood out on its typical residential avenue of early 1890 much as the first shirt-waist ensemble to appear at an afternoon tea.

The arch, plain or ornamented, pillared or unelevated, was the most borrowed Romanesque feature; it yawned over many a balcony, portico, and small front porch. Across the Bay, the arched entrance became a prime ingredient in the composite that came to be known as the "San Francisco Style." While Romanesque may not have conquered, it nonetheless left its mark front-center on many a Bay Area home.

But hands down, the most popular style of the late Victorian Era was Queen Anne, the style which rode in on the craze for quaintness. "Quaint" was the new touchstone in decoration, and the pursuit of it had become even more heated than the quest for the artistic, although

91

Crusades-inspired architecture was the chosen motif of such diversified Oakland congregations as the Sacred Heart Catholics, the First Unitarians, the First Baptists, and the First Church of Christ Scientist. Above at Twenty-first Street and Telegraph Avenue is the First Baptist Church. All four churches are still serving their congregations. *(Oakland Public Library)*

Looking like a mighty stone fortress is the shingle-covered Piedmont Baths, at right. The vogue for hygiene created a demand for the public bath. For a few cents one could buy a refreshing soak in congenial atmosphere. *(North collection)*

Houts & Ramage, dealer in masculine clothing, whose chief owners were Frank Houts and Arthur Ramage, stood at 1311-1317 Washington Street in Oakland. The building's design is a transitional one, denoting the bridge between Victorian and modern architecture. While incorporating a classical cornice with dental brackets and a Greek key frieze together with wide-arched Romanesque windows and eclectic molding, it is, nonetheless, essentially modern in its composition. Heretofore, commercial structures had tried to look like residences, affecting such ornamental details as columns, balconies and turrets, now they began to admit their utilitarian purpose. *(Albert Norman collection)*

This eye-catching Victorian at 1536 Oxford Street in Berkeley combines Queen Anne architectural features with Eastlake detailing. Typically Queen Anne is the round tower with helmet cap and finial; so is the inset balcony with low balustrade and the latticed arches of the entrance way. Eastlake shows in the decorative woodwork panels at the peaks of the two front gables, the rosetted panels between the stories, and the scrollwork encircling the tower. Note the scalloped shingles on the building's upper portion. Complementing the architectural ornamentation is the delicate wrought iron fence, believed to have been brought from New Orleans by the house's ship captain owner, Joseph Boudrow. *(Berkeley Chamber of Commerce)*

it seems to have been mostly a matter of semantics as to what was which. *Harper's Magazine* urged this new look for interiors, insisting three ingredients were mandatory: "a bunch of peacock feathers, a brass pot of cattails, and a medieval candlestick."

The notion got a big assist in the Bay Area when Oscar Wilde paid a much-publicized visit in 1882. Wilde, who first snared recognition as a lecturer on interior decoration, lectured in San Francisco and in several other California cities dressed in black velvet knee breeches, silken blouse with lace cuffs, dancing pumps, and an expression of utter ennui. *His* favorite note of quaintness was a potted sunflower, which was, however, resisted, possibly because of a local custom of planting sunflowers to disguise privies.

The style that architecturally filled the bill for quaintness was introduced to California by the *California Architect* the same year of Oscar Wilde's visit. Queen Anne was a whimsically-mixed concoction of high peaked roofs, recessed upstairs balconies, odd-shaped chimneys, bargeboards, spindled verandas, and stained glass windows. Queen Anne was also casement windows, sham half-timbering, oriels, fancy-cut shingles, decorative tiles and corner towers, variously round, square, or octagonal, topped with pointed dunce cap or bulging helmet. Obviously, combinations were almost limitless. Another English import, it was the brain child of the London architect Norman Shaw, of whom it was said that there was "hardly a style in the history books" that he did not turn to his purposes. The exception, however,

94

seems to have been the era of the gouty monarch named Anne, which favored a highly-symmetrical classicism; nobody has ever discovered the connection there.

Another secret of the style's success was that it was so accommodating. Not only did the good queen offer something to please everyone's taste, but everyone might attain it. Queen Anne might be built luxuriously or frugally, from an architect's plans or from an humble plan book. The designs adapted readily to the vernacular balloon frame method of construction, and every carpenter was up to its simple demands. It adjusted to any floor plan, from a plain rectangle to the most rambling asymmetry.

Moreover, builders found it easy to substitute local detail preferences and materials in the formula; indeed, Queen Anne had no sooner arrived in California than she received an injection of Eastlake. That is, wherever space permitted on her busy facade. Builders as blithely substituted bay windows for casements, redwood shingles for slate roofs, and stucco insets for decorative tiles. And as soon as they had mastered the style, they began

mixing it with Georgian and Romanesque. Being quaint *and* accommodating proved an irresistible combination. Queen Anne made a whirlwind conquest, winning sophisticated and rusticated alike.

Permitted so much license, it is no wonder that the queen sometimes strayed into the realm of the bizarre, and thus into ridicule. Press detractors branded the style "eccentric," "scrappy," and "a sheer affectation, altogether unworthy of the attention of grown men." One critic feared "the English house is strangling itself with the entrails of its own past glories." Two years after introducing the style, the *California Architect* ribbed it with the following imaginary dialogue between client and builder.

"The thing that puzzles me is to know what style of cottage it is. It is not Gothic, nor Italian, nor — "

"No, it is absolutely nothing. As to style, it is simply a meaningless hodge-podge, to be frank with you."

"Well, what shall I call it? Have you no name for hodge-podges?"

"Oh, yes! We call 'em Queen Annes."

This diversified six-story Berkeley structure that juggles Queen Anne, Swiss, Bavarian, and Moorish influences had an equally diversified career. Maurice Curtis, actor and theater owner, built it in 1882 intending it as a retreat for actors. But the project failed, and he used it for a time as his private residence, during which it was the scene of many bohemian parties. Later it housed a night club, then was headquarters for a candy company. In 1903, the Christian Brothers took it over and established St. Joseph's Academy boarding school. After that, it housed St. Mary's College High School. Its checkered career ended in 1959 with its demolition.

(*National Parks Service*)

But most Californians rolled out the red carpet. The style's smitten proponents hailed it as "a delightful insurrection," "expressive of the artistic quality of refined and educated minds," even called it "honest and practical," while averring it to be also picturesque, candid, cozy, and of course quaint.

The accommodating style cut a wide swath in the East Bay. The builder of wee cottage and grand mansion alike opted for cozy Queen Anne. It little mattered to a mansion owner that he might find a few blocks away a miniature replica of his dream house wedged on its tiny lot, an unblushing assembly of tiny turrets and verandas and balconies that resembled window boxes. On Queen Anne the millionaire and his valet saw eye to eye.

Samuel T. Alexander, who ruled with near feudal authority over his vast Hawaiian sugar plantations, in Oakland lived in a playful Queen Anne which was a veritable smorgasbord of divertissement. The visitor had a choice of four different entrances, each with a different treatment, while indoors he might take his pick of the "salon parlor," the "loungery," the "sitting room," or the "cozy den." To ascend to one of the four upper floors, he mounted a winding staircase that curved five times within a circular tower bathed in a kaleidoscope of light filtered through multiple stained-glass windows. While dining, he was cheered by a huge fireplace banded by vast white stone slabs, the topmost bearing the incised Hawaiian salutation "Aloha, nui."

Oakland brick mogul Peter Remillard, inventor of a new brick process, built a combination Stick-Eastlake-Queen Anne, which may or may not have been the model for the fictional Morse mansion in *Martin Eden*. A childhood friend of Remillard's daughter Lillian recalls that Lillian once acted as tutor for the young Jack London. She later went to New York to study music under Walter Damrosche, sang at the Metropolitan Opera, and married Count Alesandro Dandini di Cesena, scion of one of Italy's oldest families. The countess spent her later years in Hillsborough, presiding over the ninety-two-room Chateau Carolans.

On a sixty-five-acre estate in the south Berkeley hills, near the present location of the Claremont Hotel, Judge John Garber built a palatial

For his "mainland retreat," the Hawaiian sugar king Samuel Thomas Alexander built this fanciful Stick-Eastlake-Queen Anne house at the corner of Oakland's Sixteenth and Filbert Streets. The architect made lavish use of color with the art-glass windows and colored tile in entrance vestibules and in fireplaces. The staircase in the inset tower made five turns. *(Albert Norman collection)*

Whimsical Queen Anne and solemn Gothic were wed in the design of this mansion situated on a sixty-five-acre private park in the south Berkeley hills. The home of Judge John Garber, it was an important social mecca, especially for the culturati and the University set. Nearly every room had its handsome fireplace with imported decorative tiles on hearth and fireplace front. Stained-glass windows illuminated the gigantic Gothic staircase at the foot of which stood a tall grandfather's clock. A huge oak table and a giant sideboard carved in a fruit design dominated the dining room with its lofty Gothic ceiling. *(Bancroft Library)*

Victorians were avid collectors of practically everything, and much of their aggregation was channeled into specialized albums, the perusal of which was a sanctioned parlor pastime. In the 1870s, it was popular to keep scrapbooks of trade cards, an early advertising medium born of the new process of lithography. Business firms distributed glossy, bright-colored cards to all comers, who were delighted to receive them, for mass-produced color prints were still a novelty. Like the greeting cards of the day, trade cards were of endless variety, but most fell into three classifications: the sentimental, the humorous, and the romantic. An example of each was taken from the collection kept by an Oakland young lady. The embossed lacework card with carnation motif was handed out by the George Haas Candy Co. of San Francisco; W. H. Nolan & Co., Fine Shoes, of 1971 Broadway in Oakland represented itself with the artist with the reluctant bovine model; while the mustachioed gallant and his demure companion was a reminder of Roos Brothers of San Francisco. *(North collection)*

98

During the Victorian era, young and old alike attended Sunday School, and in summer flocked to Vacation Bible School. Attendance was monitored with gold stars and rewarded with a handsome merit card for one's scrapbook. *(North collection)*

Nothing on earth was so reverenced as home and mother. This postcard at left honors both.

The religious strain was one of the strongest in the Victorian character. Many popular novels had a religious theme, and the most prolific publisher in the United States was the American Tract Society. Moreover, friends sent each other decorated postcards that quoted Bible verses, such as this one.

This 1893 view of Berkeley's Shattuck Avenue, pointing south from Berkeley Way, most likely was snapped on an early Sunday morning. Weekdays the district was lively. Berkeley was experiencing a brisk population influx, sparked by the installation two years before of fast electric train service. (*Albert Norman collection*)

Queen Anne mansion; when it was completed in 1888, he christened it "Belle Rose" in memory of his Alabama childhood. The frame house had a slim, round, very-pointed tower and balustraded upstairs balconies. But it also had frothy Gothic detailing at the roof line and Gothic bargeboards in its several gables, this possibly being added to complement what the judge planned for the inside.

Exquisitely-wrought Gothic appointments, both finishing and furnishings, abounded throughout the many-corridored interior. Especially admired were the Gothic staircase of hand-carved walnut, the august dark-paneled library with its rare hand-tooled volumes, and the baronial dining room with sixteen-foot ceiling. Sir Walter Scott would have felt at home there, as did the coterie of scholarly friends the judge was fond of entertaining. Belle Rose maintained continuing hospi-

tality, including a cellar of vintage wines, for such early University of California notables as John and Joseph LeConte and Josiah Royce, and eminent California pioneers like William T. Coleman and Dr. Paolo De Vecchia. Judge Garber's spikey Gothic library furniture is owned today by the Oakland Museum, where it lends atmosphere for a collection of Victorian paintings.

The captain of a Nova Scotia windjammer was the first master of a relatively dignified three-story Queen Anne which still stands in good repair at 1536 Oxford Street in Berkeley, although it but narrowly was saved from the wreckers in 1970 when an admirer bought it to preserve it. Captain Joseph Hart Boudrow built it in 1889, surrounding it with a vast garden given mainly to pelargoniums, and enclosed it with a decorative iron fence, said to have been brought from New Orleans. Rarely used today is the steep stairway leading to the round, cone-topped corner tower, but when in port the captain climbed it often to watch his ship at anchor. Still giving good service and delight to visitors is the immense copper bathtub, nearly four feet deep, in the first floor bathroom.

Samuel Newsome, the second Newsome brother, chose a restrained Queen Anne for his new residence in expanding East Oakland. He endowed it with an overhanging Swiss porch, thus enriching the repertoire of Queen Anne options. In a plan book published by the Newsome brothers in 1890, one Queen Anne model named "Tamalpais" was characterized as an "Oakland suburban style." The most striking feature of the house, a three-story, was a highly complex shingled roof which sometimes ended at the top of the third floor, sometimes reached down to the second and at others dipped to the top of the first floor. It rather reminded one of chocolate syrup spilling over a vanilla ice cream sundae, although the designer may have had in mind the shaggy thatched roof of Elizabethan times. This whimsical roof, which seems to have been a local invention, was copied rather widely in Oakland and Berkeley. The roof of one such Berkeley house was painted bright orange.

Queen Anne even accommodated herself to a California cattle ranch. South of Oakland, beyond Hayward, was Arden Wood, the ranch home of the George W. Pattersons. As its elegant name suggests, this Queen Anne made no concession to its masculine setting. It was romantically endowed with jewel-toned stained glass windows, inset bal-

The Berkeley residential district below San Pablo Avenue and centered around Dwight Way has numerous small frame houses of interesting design and skilled workmanship. Many were built by the lumberman and contractor Niehaus. This fusion of Stick-Eastlake and Queen Anne at 839 Channing Way stands out for its original tower and its charming scrollwork panels, some depicting the sunflower. (T. W. Tenney)

conies, and a tower encircled with a floral frieze in moulded terra cotta. Also worked into the scheme were several Romanesque arches. Serving as a buffer zone between the mansion and the working ranch was a twenty-acre deer park in which sixteen of the graceful creatures roamed at leisure over a pampered green.

On Alameda's fashionable West Side, San Francisco insurance executive Henry K. Field built a twenty-four-room Queen Anne, locating it near the end of Magnolia-shaded Paru Street, so that he might be within walking distance of his yacht anchored nearby. A frequent visitor to the Field home and yacht was his celebrated cousin, the Denver poet Eugene Field. Like many another Alameda Queen Anne, the former Field home is still serving occupants well today.

Also shrugging off time, as well as retaining its unique identity, is an Alameda Queen Anne widely known as the "honeymoon cottage." The ample cottage is an openly coquettish Queen Anne in rustic shingle in which the designer let out all stops with a helmeted tower, arched inset balconies, lower curved veranda with spindles and upper curved veranda with grill. Here are all the curves and bulges to which the public became so accustomed that they complained that succeeding styles were "flat-chested."

The well-known legend stems from the original owners. She was a New York society girl, he a handsome Central Pacific railroad conductor, and they met on a train when she was traveling West in the late 1880s. Seemingly, railroad conductors then had much the same glamour airline pilots do today. The trip lasted several days, during which the couple fell in love; by the time they reached California they had decided to get married. Not long after, they built their shingled cottage at the end of his line. But Alamedans say that after a few years they sold their house and left town. Nobody can remember why.

All this exuberance — and in some cases excess — was born happily out of irrepressible optimism.

For it was a time of economic prosperity and national tranquility. Nothing really bad had happened since the Civil War, and that dreadful holocaust had shaken the West Coast far less than the rest of the country. It was generally agreed that people were becoming better and wiser, laws and rulers were becoming more just, music was sweeter, and art purer. Above all, people were becoming more tasteful; on all sides sensibilities were being sharpened. One writer, extolling the heights to which residential architecture and interior decoration had ascended, assured her readers they were living in a "fine summer of perfected art."

Yet these styles of the 1880s and early 1890s — Eastlake, Byzantine, Romanesque, and Queen Anne — which never diluted themselves with inhibitions and which, as a result, were alternately so beautiful and so grotesque, are the Victorian styles which later on would draw the heaviest obloquy. Even the finest examples of the styles went almost totally unappreciated for a time; all were disdainfully lumped together (with the exception of Romanesque public architecture) as representing a "collapse of taste" and the "dark ages of architecture."

The architects who designed them and their clients who commissioned them would never have believed it possible. Of course, the styles had their detractors even then, but the majority of Victorians, like Martin Eden, greatly enjoyed and admired them. After all, the people who lived in these houses remembered their years as the "Elegant Eighties."

Curiously, the style that was to become the most reviled of all not only won the widest popularity during its flowering but would enjoy the longest run. The ghost of the accommodating Queen Anne lingered into the second decade of the Twentieth Century. On the eve of the First World War, California plan book editors still were recommending Queen Anne designs with candle snuffer turrets and haphazard dormers for their freedom, charm, and coziness.

In the Elegant Eighties, this Queen Anne mansion stood on Oakland's fashionable Alice Street, the home of the A. A. Pennoyer family of the Taft and Pennoyer Department Store. Scion Richard Pennoyer studied law at Harvard and married an Eastern belle who was the granddaughter of financier J. P. Morgan. (*Albert Norman collection*)

Cemeteries ranked high in importance with Victorians and were visited often. Oakland's Mountain View Cemetery grew out of a meeting of some town leaders on December 26, 1863, in the local telegraph office. To plan the two-hundred-acre site, they engaged America's leading landscape architect Frederick Law Olmsted, who laid it out like an ornamental park. The tombstones of the era, chiseled by local stonecutters, reflect the Classic, Gothic, French and Egyptian influences that prevailed in architecture. The infant tomb inscribed "Our Babies," from a San Leandro cemetery, is in the French style, which resembled a bed which served as a flower planter. Gothic and Classic styles are combined in the monumental Stenzel tomb, while the Dougherty burial plot features Egyptian obelisks. Dr. Sam Merritt, one of the organizers of Mountain View, lies buried there in a mausoleum with Egyptian motif. *(Opposite page, above, Louis Stein collection, below, Oakland* TRIBUNE; *this page, above, Oakland* TRIBUNE, *below, Albert Norman collection)*

105

A view of the Main Hall at Arbor Villa includes a glimpse of the famous pipe organ that contributed its part to the grand living style at the estate of the borax millionaire F. M. Smith. Organ concerts for invited guests were part of the almost continual round of entertaining at the mansion. Smith conducted a world-wide search for the rare woods used in the elaborate paneling and parquet floors of the interiors. *(Oakland Public Library)*

106

Countesses and Conveniences

"The Oakland lassie — she drives papa to the train, she goes to college, she belongs to charities innumerable, drifting most often across the bay, looking as though she had stepped from a book, the up-to-date Gibson girl." Thus did "Roxie," popular society columnist for the Oakland weekly *Saturday Night* ("A journal for Sunday Reading") characterize the typical East Bay debutante of the Nineties.

The East Bay not only had arrived in the realm of culture and finance, but was traveling in the highest reaches of society. Young womankind, it has been said, is society's finest flower, and East Bay belles, during the late Victorian Era, were cutting a most impressive swath. Not only on the West Coast social scene, but on the highly competitive stage of Europe. A present-day contributor to "The Knave" column of the Oakland *Tribune*, observed not long ago, recalling those years, that "more of Oakland's fair daughters (had) married into the European aristocracy than those of any other city on the Pacific Coast. Marie Sourdry married French Count de Began de Larzourie, Lelia Kirkham, daughter of General Kirkham, became the English Lady Yard-Buller, Maude Burke, niece of Horace Carpentier . . . became Lady Bache-Cunard. While on a tour of the World, Lord Sholto-Douglas took a fancy to Oakland, married one of our girls and settled down here for several years. West Oakland's Gertrude Dermott became Lady Forbes-Robertson. Italy furnished three titles in Lillian Remillard, who became Countess Dandini di Cesena; Alla Henshaw, the Princess Zurlo, and Adele Chevalier, the Countess Cipollina."

These fetching creatures, who looked like book illustrations and were turning royal heads, had been as carefully nurtured as the hybrid camellias in their fathers' conservatories. Their social graces had been perfected in the East Bay's proper parlors and ballrooms, especially in the exclusive assemblies of the august Cotillion Club. East Bay society then divided into several centers: the Jackson Street set, composed of the prominent families residing around Lake Merritt; the set from beautiful oak-lined Adeline Street; the Market Street set; and those in Piedmont, Alameda, and Berkeley. Each set had its own busy social orbit, but these were linked by the Cotillion Club and its series of gala winter balls. Another contributor to the The Knave recalled: "Here they all met each year at a ball and danced throughout the winter. . . . Invitations were much sought after; and all passed upon by a committee. To belong to the organization, your social position was firmly established, and you were numbered among the elite of the community."

With such cultivated society in her midst, the former New York socialite in her "honeymoon cottage" in Alameda could scarcely have languished

This view of Arbor Villa ballroom recalls the gala Cotillion Club balls. As remembered by Arthur McPhail, "The main event of the evening was the Grand March . . . It took considerable skill to be able to move the crowd in maneuvers and keep the Grand March moving. If you were chosen to lead, and the crowd got confused, it was a reflection on your ability. You were never asked to be the leader again. To improvise something new each time was also something that reflected honor on a man . . . At the end of the Grand March when the crowd broke up into a waltz and your leadership was crowned with success, it was a grand and glorious feeling." (Jane Voiles collection)

After making a fortune with his Twenty Mule Team borax refinery in Alameda, F. M. Smith in 1893 set himself up in splendor in this forty-two-room pseudo Elizabethan mansion, the design of Walter Matthews. But to remind him of his humble origins, he moved onto the grounds the shack he had occupied while prospecting at Teel's Marsh, Nevada, where he made his borax strike. The contrast between shack and mansion created a local Horatio Alger legend. However, Smith's fortune, together with the legend, suffered a collapse in 1912, when he was forced to sign over his holdings to creditors. He was beginning to make a comeback in borax when he died. *(Oakland Public Library)*

---

for want of fashionable diversions and amenities. Indeed, Alameda considered itself something of a Newport, but with added urban advantages. Tennis courts and cricket courts abounded everywhere; the glistening bathing beaches on the then unpolluted Bay were the finest in the whole area. Just beyond the city limits the Gentleman's Driving Association maintained a splendid race track.

What's more, with excellent yacht harbors on both sides of the peninsula, Alameda was a magnet for yachtsmen. Its Encinal Club on the southern shore boasted the most imposing boathouse in California. Among yachts moored in the Estuary was that of Frank M. Smith whose borax factory in Alameda was the biggest borax supplier in the world. Smith's yacht had stood up victoriously against those of English royalty. Another was the yacht *Casco*, owned by Dr. Merritt, who in mellow retirement lived the life of a million-aire sportsman, frequently piloting his stately one hundred-foot vessel in regattas along the Eastern Seaboard. The *Casco* had acquired a literary cachet in 1888 when Robert Louis Stevenson and his wife, the former Fanny Osbourne, leased it for their storied cruise among the South Sea Islands, from which Fanny returned heartbroken, after burying her frail genius on Samoa.

The popular journalist Thomas Nunan, writing in the April, 1894, monthly *Californian Illustrated*, observed of Alameda: "The rural quiet, the happy home life in an entire change of surroundings and atmosphere, attract a most desirable class of citizens." Alameda was the only municipality in the Bay Area where residences might be built right on the water. So numerous were millionaire menages on the elegant, leafy West Side, it was being called the "Gold Coast." Many Northern Californians maintained week-end houses there. But with

Anyone for bowling, billiards or boxing? Male guests had their choice in the basement recreation room at Arbor Villa. *(Oakland Public Library)*

the crack ferry commuter service, anybody who wished to could remain there year around, and more and more of those exposed to Alameda's multiple charms so preferred.

Since losing the railroad terminal, Alameda had studiously cultivated a tone of elegant rusticism, battling to keep at bay the "undesirable features of city life." Alamedans went in for horticultural contests and save-that-tree and plant-a-tree campaigns, while city ordinance promoted the garden atmosphere with a requirement that houses be given a fifty-foot frontage and generous setback. Anything smacking of industry was imperiously waved away, and city fathers kept the small business district wedged within a narrow confine — smotheringly so, businessmen complained. M. W. Wood in his *History of Alameda County* published in 1883 noted approvingly that Alameda had "not gone ahead too fast" like some other communities and that it did "not catch so many peddlers, beggars, tramps and other social abominations as towns which are on main-trav-

eled railroads or thoroughfares." In its official brochure, Alameda boasted of being a place that had "not been disturbed" and quite confidently designated itself "the society suburb."

Of course, the object of Alameda's half-congratulatory, half-envious claims and comparisons was Oakland, the purloiner of its railroad terminal. Certainly, Oakland hadn't been shunning commerce; its new Board of Trade had been assiduously courting it. And with dazzling success. By the mid-1880s, it had risen to the position of second city on the Pacific Coast in manufactures, which hired more than 3,000 people. The Oakland *Weekly Times* was headily predicting that what with the harbor improvements then underway "Oakland is bound to be the greatest city of the Pacific Coast."

Business was brisk in the smart shops of the impressive commercial district, rapidly expanding with substantial buildings of brick, stone, and cast-iron. Lobbies of the twelve principal hotels were milling with drummers and business repre-

110

sentatives from Chicago and the East. Vigorous advertising finally had disabused East Bay residents of the persistent notion that to get "the latest" one had to cross the Bay. On Saturday night, when stores, offices and restaurants stayed open until nearly midnight and practically everybody put in his appearance on Broadway, Oakland downtown was a teeming mass of human acquisitiveness and gregariousness. Foot and vehicle traffic grew so congested that in 1890 Oakland had to pass an ordinance limiting carriages and other horse-drawn vehicles to a speed of five miles per hour, three miles per at intersections.

No longer did San Francisco business writers refer to "our metropolitan offshoot Oakland." Oakland now had its own satellite towns. Indeed, to hear Oakland tell it San Francisco had become dependent on Oakland for *its* prosperity. Oakland press and real estate circles agreed the city's rapid population growth was due primarily to the "large

number of arrivals from the East," instead of to the "spill of its neighbor." In the opinion of the Oakland *Enquirer*, those attracted to Lotus Land benefited San Francisco in this way: "Many of capital, who seek for their families such climatic and social and educational advantages as Oakland has, come here and buy and build those charming houses for which the city is noted and, finding it all that can be wished for a home, then carry some of their capital to San Francisco and add it to her mercantile wealth and energies . . . San Francisco would not be so busy were it not for Oakland."

Housing all the newcomers kept real estate operations brisk. To fill immediate needs, realtors kept a large number of rental cottages changing hands. In some blocks of Oakland all of the offices were filled with real estate agents or dealers. The construction of the San Pablo Avenue cable road opened up inviting new residential tracts along its line; at one land auction buyers grabbed up

---

Robert Louis Stevenson, who had left Oakland in 1880 an unknown, returned to the Bay Area in 1888 a celebrated literary figure. "I know a little about fame now," he was quoted as saying, "and it is no good compared to a yacht." He had just chartered Dr. Sam Merritt's yacht "Casco" for a cruise to the South Seas. Before the sailing,

Dr. Merritt, bearded in background, posed with the yachting party that included Dora Van de Grift, Stevenson's sister-in-law; Mrs. Margaret Stevenson, his mother; and Fanny Osbourne Stevenson, his wife. Stevenson stands at right. *(Jane Voiles collection)*

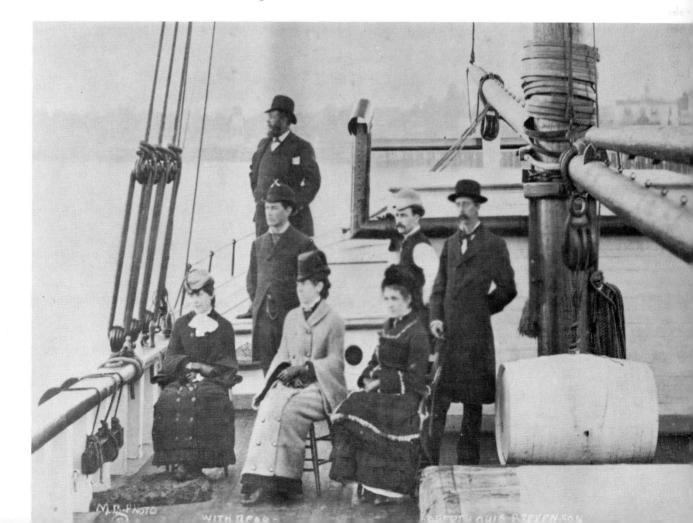

Beginning in the 1870s and continuing for several decades, much of the responsibility of East Bay housekeeping could be left to a "Number One Boy." The transcontinental railroad completed, Chinese workers migrated back to the Coast, many becoming skilled household servants. They partly shaved their heads, winding a braided queue around the crown, and on ordinary days wore long white blouses and black trousers. For special occasions they dressed splendidly. Recalls a contributor to the Oakland *Tribune:* "I can see our Louie in his turquoise blue coat, trousers of creamy pongee, soft embroidered shoes and snowy linen apron, serving refreshments to callers on New Year's Day." *(Society of California Pioneers)*

The homey cast-iron range was a fixture of most kitchens throughout the Victorian Era. A gas range was introduced in Oakland in the 1880s without success. A clumsy electric range was exhibited at the World's Fair of 1892. *(Oakland Public Library)*

ALF BRUSETH
574-22nd STR OAK.

This early version of an apartment house, a circa 1895 four-plex, stood at 570-576 Twenty-Second Street, serving Oakland families until its demolition in 1965. The side entrances admitted to the first floor; center doors led to the second. American apartment houses evolved in the late Victorian Era. First called "French flats," after the multiple-dwellings constructed in Paris around 1850, the housing form that was to characterize the American city was at first highly controversial. Critics argued it was immoral and unhealthy to house several families under one roof.

113

sixty-three parcels of San Pablo Avenue real estate. In Oakland, in 1890, more than 500 new homes collectively worth $2,000,000 went up, seventy of them in the popular new Kennedy Tract.

Piedmont's growth was sparked by the completion, in 1890, of its new cable line to Oakland. The ambitious suburb already had made an impressive start at collecting millionaires, who by the century's end would number thirty-two, giving Piedmont the largest per capita wealth of any community of its size in the United States. The line was scarcely completed when the route, a former country road, began building up with modest-sized homes, which soon would form a solid urban chain. These new car lines, both cable and electric, were a potent magnet for residences in those pre-automobile days. Open space was rapidly disappearing and the transition between suburb and town becoming less and less perceptible. The East Bay was becoming homogenized.

The northern suburbs of Golden Gate, Newbury, and Lorin (soon to be annexed to Berkeley)

were building up. However, a transportation bottleneck had stunted Berkeley; after its growth spurt in the 1870s, it had slowed and its population had scarcely passed the 5,000 mark in the 1890 census. Its civic boasts, instead, were for its culture and its "select society." In addition to academicians, its citizenry was liberally sprinkled with bankers, lawyers, physicians, and capitalists, whose business interests were either in San Francisco or in Oakland, but who preferred to live in a scholarly atmosphere.

Then, in 1891, came completion of the electric road, the Oakland & Berkeley Rapid Transit Company, first of its kind west of the Mississippi River. This swift, glistening train, which connected with commodious passenger ferries in Oakland, took the tedium out of commuting. It also set off a population influx that would nearly double the population within four years. Berkeley's village days were over.

The new Claremont suburb was situated on a canyon-edged meadow in the south Berkeley

Harvest sales were drawing hurrying customers on the afternoon in the late 1890s when this photograph, at left, was snapped at Oakland's Twelfth and Washington Streets. Providing transportation were the electric trolley, horse-drawn carriages and wagons, and bicycles, but there's not an automobile in sight. In the background is the Oakland City Hall that was supplanted by the present one in 1914. (*Albert Norman collection*)

This airy vehicle was Henry Caseholt's experimental overhead cable car that ran for four months along Highland Avenue in Piedmont. While the car ran on the tracks of the Consolidated Cable Company, it was pulled by an overhead cable that ran through sheaves attached to posts. But the satisfactory performance of the conventional underground cable coupled with feeling against unsightly overhead posts made it impossible for Caseholt to find a backer. He is pictured at the controls, and Mark Requa, one of the line's owners, is pictured in background in straw hat. For a thirteen-year period, beginning in 1886, Oakland had cable car service equal to San Francisco's. The cables kept spinning until 1899, when the lines were converted to electricity. (*Albert Norman collection*)

hills, bordering Judge Garber's estate. Its planner was John Galen Howard, the new supervisor of planning for the University of California and its first professor of architecture. Claremont initiated a new type of exclusiveness with its elaborate entrance gates, restrictions against apartments or businesses, and firm requirements on building expenditure and ground ratio. Its streets and those of other new hillside developments were laid out to curve with hill contours, instead of being forced into the gridiron plan so ruinously followed in San Francisco. The pleasantly serpentine avenues were given picturesque names like Cragmont, Rockridge, and Wildwood. Berkeley homes were becoming known for their velvety lawns, pampered borders, and thriving rose gardens.

Another kind of progress in East Bay living had been taking place. Some marvelous things had been happening in household modernization. The Nineteenth Century brought more revolutionary changes in the area of home convenience and comfort than in any century ever before, and in the late Victorian Era change was introduced almost daily, generating ecstatic excitement in women's magazines. East Bay matrons were avid readers of Eastern journals and demanded these innovations at once.

Consider communication advances. To replace the swarms of messenger boys scurrying about the town with sealed envelopes in the 1870s, the American District Telephone Company had installed a system of call boxes in Oakland and Alameda residences and businesses. If incapable of transmitting speech, the impressive metal box with moveable hands could be made to summon service by pointing the hand to the number for police, fire department, doctor, carriage, dray, etc. A buzz registered at the telegraph office, which relayed the call to the proper party.

Oakland's call boxes had seemed miraculous until Dr. Alexander Graham Bell, in 1876, in Philadelphia, demonstrated the superiority of his invention by shouting over its charged wire: "Dr. Watson, come here, I want you." Two years later the East Bay was shouting over its own telephones, and consulting the latest home journals for tips on telephone etiquette. One of the first demonstration sets was installed at the Isaac Requa mansion in Piedmont, where excited

groups gathered each evening to listen in pindrop silence while Mr. Requa "rang up" San Francisco.

For some time, however, telephones remained more entertaining than assisting, because of their irksome unreliability. It was something of a game deciphering what one's telephone contact had really said over the crackling transmitter. Besides, the intriguing instrument was out of order as much as in, one of the plaguing problems being the affinity of the line paraphernalia for California fog; when the line became saturated with dampness, it went dead until the sun revived it. Call box subscriptions remained steady until the telephone company came up with fog-proof insulation.

When the telephone company delayed in extending service to Berkeley's scattered population, Berkeleyans collected funds and installed their own poles and lines to hook up with the Oakland exchange. Then after a dearth of attention from the telephone interests, Berkeley was plagued by too much. Two rival companies set up business there in the 1890s, causing a snarl of complication. Not only did householders have to decide which service to subscribe to, but businesses were obliged to subscribe to both and to list two sets of numbers. Confusion mounted until one company bought the other out.

For indoor communication some houses were equipped with speaking tubes located in strategic places. The William de Fremery house in Oakland had a ship-type system of one-inch diameter tubes that ran throughout the three-story house. With the introduction of electric service in the 1880s, housekeeping was greatly assisted with electrical bells and buzzers, especially installed at front doors, between parlor and kitchen, and under the dining table within reach of the hostess' toe. Many houses were equipped with a strangelooking device called an "announciator," which could be made to summon any member of the household staff to any room in the house.

A dazzling succession of household wonders were pouring in, at once simplifying and complicating existence. These work- and time-saving temptations included sewing machines, washing machines, mechanical churns, mechanical ice cream freezers, mechanical carpet sweepers. The

Horsecar after horsecar switched to electric power. Here Berkeley's Grove Street trolley pauses before the First Congregational Church. In the mid-1890s, the East Bay was credited with the finest electric car system in the nation. Commuters kept trains and ferries so busy that San Francisco firms, alarmed over the exodus, ordered their employees not to reside in the East Bay. The decree proved unenforceable. (*Louis Stein collection*)

This northward view of Shattuck Avenue at Berkeley Station was made when downtown Berkeley was served by both a steam train and F. M. Smith's Key System electric cars. Note how the Key System tracks angled off, thus creating Shattuck Square and Berkeley Square. The Key System provided the fastest route to San Francisco — only thirty-five minutes from Berkeley Station to the Ferry Building — and in time put the steam train out of business. (*Berkeley Firefighters Association*)

Former habitues of the old Forum Bar on Oakland's Broadway must have blinked in wonder when they sauntered in for a tot of whiskey to find the place had been converted into a fashionable haberdashery. For old time's sake, the new management, Lynn Stanley's Haberdashery, had left champagne buckets and beer mugs scattered about as novel decor, while also retaining the old bar rail for the convenience of customers perusing galluses and collar buttons. *(Albert Norman collection)*

---

new wire window screens saved time from swatting flies and raising and lowering the bedroom mosquito nets that had been a staple in East Bay homes. An Oakland architect incorporated a laundry chute into one of his designs, prompting envy and imitation.

While every new modernizing fixture was an exciting conversation piece, there was the vexing problem of getting used to the thing and of explaining it to the servants. In switching from kerosene to gas jets, users had had to learn that to blow out the flame subjected one to the danger of explosion or asphyxiation. Downtown Oakland hotels had posted signs "DON'T BLOW OUT THE LIGHTS!" Once that was learned, next

everybody had to become accustomed to the puzzling incandescent electric light.

Besides, there was the baffling decision as to whether to invest in gas or electrical fixtures. Many houses had both power systems, but what with the companies competing heatedly for business, one might edge the other out and leave one with a bag of useless equipment. How was one to know? The gas light's flickering flame had seemed on its way out after the invention of the electric light, but with the coming of the flame-steadying gas mantel in 1884, gaslight had taken on a new flourish. The forward-looking Oakland Gas Company, first gas works in this country to install high-pressure gas, in the 1880s introduced the gas

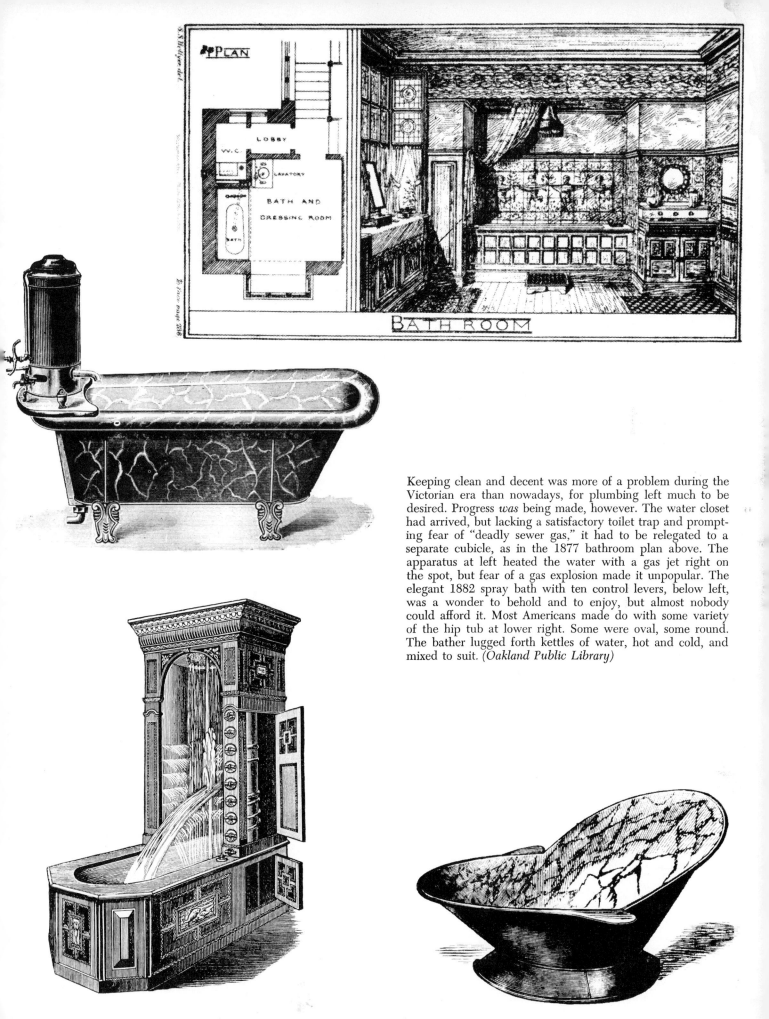

BATHROOM

Keeping clean and decent was more of a problem during the Victorian era than nowadays, for plumbing left much to be desired. Progress *was* being made, however. The water closet had arrived, but lacking a satisfactory toilet trap and prompting fear of "deadly sewer gas," it had to be relegated to a separate cubicle, as in the 1877 bathroom plan above. The apparatus at left heated the water with a gas jet right on the spot, but fear of a gas explosion made it unpopular. The elegant 1882 spray bath with ten control levers, below left, was a wonder to behold and to enjoy, but almost nobody could afford it. Most Americans made do with some variety of the hip tub at lower right. Some were oval, some round. The bather lugged forth kettles of water, hot and cold, and mixed to suit. *(Oakland Public Library)*

Pedestal Tip-up Lavatory, 1890

THE POTTER'S ART

Practicality wasn't the only consideration in bathroom design. Those who could afford it demanded that the room also be artistic. The arts of both sculpture and painting were brought to bear, as demonstrated in these plumbing fixtures from throughout the Victorian Era. Receptacles were imprinted both inside and out with figures that ranged from geometric designs, such as the Greek key bowl on couchant lion, to delicate Dresden china flower figures, as on bathtub at left. Favored too were the pop art of the period and realistic historical scenes. The ocean provided sculptural inspiration for the water closet in dolphin and shell motif at lower left. But strictly utilitarian was the apparatus below. It is a vapour bath that could be purchased from a mail order house for about five dollars. In parts of the West where water was scarce, it had a long run of popularity. *(Oakland Public Library)*

'The Dolphin', 1882

120

kitchen range to the West. The firm's superintendent Joseph Eastland had been to Europe and returned with an inventory of Fletcher Stoves. The new gas range proved a flop locally, however. Women who purchased the stoves for their cooks to use often found themselves presiding over them, through necessity. Servants shied from them as though from a powder keg and were prone to depart the household that acquired one, sometimes without giving notice.

But the most dramatic advance was in plumbing. At the mid-century, the East Bay's squatter towns had had to rely on the privy. But then so did New York City. The water closet hadn't yet caught on in America, even though an Englishman had invented it in 1596. Indoors, the middleclass still had its chamber pot under the bed, and the best the rich could manage was the portable commode, sometimes camouflaged as a bookcase, which servants trundled out from time to time. Since sewers hadn't arrived yet either, the commode had to be emptied in cesspool or gutter, along with water from the tin bathtub and porcelain washbasin on the bedroom washstand.

But with the availability of metal pipe, the water closet moved in swiftly in the 1860s, and the hygienic splash from its chain-operated overhead tank was heard across the land. New and expanding towns, unencumbered by old sanitary systems, could introduce certain plumbing innovations more rapidly than the older cities; thus East Bay plumbing generally kept abreast of the East Coast. Cold tap kitchen sinks and downstairs washbasins multiplied along with water closets, all supplied with water from well or cistern. All drained into a cesspool in the back yard. Cold tap wooden bathtubs lined with zinc or copper were sometimes installed downstairs where room could be found. Hot water for tub and sink came from a kettle heated on the kitchen stove.

And no sooner had running water moved indoors than its delighted users began trying to coax it upstairs. In pre-public-water days, this wasn't easy. But by applying considerable labor to a hand-worked force pump, a modest water supply could be elevated to a roof cistern or upstairs tank. This source permitted a water closet to be installed in a cubicle off the upstairs hall and a cold tap basin in the master bedroom. Sometimes the force pump was made to supply an upstairs bathtub, but the task of carrying kettles of hot water upstairs rather discouraged its use.

The laborious process of keeping upstairs tanks filled was relieved for some Oaklanders in 1867, when they were able to connect to Anthony Chabot's new water system, supplied by the Lake Temescal reservoir. When connections remained low due to the high cost, the city sought to boost them by placing a tax on windmills; but angry windmill owners accused the water company of instigating the tax to kill off competition and the council was forced to rescind its action. Brass hot water heaters came on the market, permitting the addition of hot-water taps. When James LaRue, ferryboat magnate, built a new mansion in Oakland in 1872, he installed two hot-and-cold running bathtubs, upstairs and down.

Most of these plumbing changes were effected to the tune of passionate controversy. Bringing the privy indoors was felt by many to be a grave mistake. It was sure to spread contagion, or "deadly sewer gas" would belch up from the drain and asphyxiate you. Sewer gas was believed to be the source of diphtheria and numerous other diseases. The press took it up. Some editors urged that all plumbing be ripped from the house before it was too late. Warned the Oakland *Weekly Times* in 1886: "So fatal are the return gases from a drain that it is safer to keep up the old country custom of bowl and pitcher . . ." Another local writer averred that "whether a man, woman, or child is deprived of life through the agency of deadly drugs, the pistol, knife, or badly constructed sewers, the effect is the same upon the death-stricken individual." It was even claimed that due to the menace "multitudes have found early and untimely repose in death . . ." It was as a precaution against sewer gas that water closets were installed in their own separate cubicles, without direct access to bedrooms or bathrooms.

In retrospect, the danger seems to have been exaggerated. Today one searches fruitlessly for recorded deaths definitely attributed to sewer gas asphyxiation. Could the alarm have been spread, spitefully, by envious water closet have-nots? That the drains were a source of obnoxious odors is well documented, however, and this problem persisted even after Oakland installed its expensive new sewer system in the 1880s. Alameda reported marked improvement with its new sewer system, in which it took enormous pride. Its main sewer lines were flushed twice daily with salt water, while branch lines were given hourly flushings by an automatic tipping tank devised by an Alameda citizen. Nonetheless, a completely satisfactory routing of sewer gas would await the invention in the Twentieth Century of a really workable toilet trap. The danger of the early bathroom water heater was a more ascertainable peril. They not infrequently blew up with terrifying results.

Despite the nay-saying, plumbing conquered. It required but one generation of use to be considered an absolute necessity for gracious living. Indeed, by the late Victorian Era, plumbing, together with central heating, lighting, and communication features, had come to be almost as important — and as expensive — as a building's structure.

The largest single expense was the bathroom, which had risen in more ways than one. Rechristened the toilet after the French *toilette*, the water closet frequently was enlivened with imprinted decoration that covered the entire porcelain area. Floral and geometric designs were favored. Popular in the East Bay was a model named "Supreme" that was decorated with Grecian scrolls and acanthus leaves and had a polished mahogany seat. Its manufacturer was the Joseph Budde Company of San Francisco, which had another big seller called "Pioneer," possibly designed for a daily reminder of how fast the West was progressing. It depicted scenes of crossing the plains to California: Conestoga wagons in procession, gun-carrying men on horseback, Indians war dancing around a campfire, and so on. Budde advertisements featured two other decorated models called "Cliff Stream" and "Ocean Spray" and boasted of having received "a medal and diploma at the State Fair in 1888 and 1889." Interestingly, these aesthetic names failed to catch on with the public, whereas a less descriptive trade name "John Douglas" — or part of it — seems to have found a permanent place in the English language.

The Joseph Budde Company waged a subtle advertising campaign to persuade the public that its water closets were both sweeter-smelling and safer than those of its competitors. The medium was two eye-catching calendars which received wide circulation in the Bay Area. One depicted a voluptuous damsel about to strip for her bath; although standing beside a water closet her blissful expression dispelled any hint of offensive odor. The other version portrayed an innocent-faced child wrapped in her bathrobe, implying the innocency of any obnoxious gases of the adjacent "Cyclone" model water closet.

As the water closet became more decorative it was given a larger, more attractive cubicle, and finally was united with the bathtub in one sizable room. *Picturesque Homes of California*, 1890 edition, observed: "Much artistic skill is now being spent in the construction of fine bathrooms. In large residences they are now splendid apartments, almost suggestive of old Roman days." The editor recommended that they be no smaller than six-by-eight-feet in a small house and ten-by-twelve in a large one. The nobbiest of these splendid bathing salons were equipped with sofas, console tables, oriental rugs, stained glass windows, and gilded swinging mirrors, in which the privy would never have recognized itself.

Naturally, all this comfort and splendor couldn't fail to encourage personal hygiene, an improvement that was long overdue. It is sometimes forgotten how modern regular bathing is. The human animal in his long march to civilization was astonishingly late in acquiring the habit of personal cleanliness. Queen Isabella, America's sponsor, so to speak, disclosed late in life that she had had only two baths — one the day she was born and one the day she married Ferdinand. Our early American ancestors probably were scarcely more fastidious.

However, by the mid-nineteenth century bathing had caught on to the degree that it was considered a good thing to take a weekly bath, and in the East Bay the most popular bathtub was a cavernous affair with lion claw feet called the "Independent Tub." Saturday night was felt to be the appropriate time for the weekly scrubbing. However, by no means everybody bathed so often, and bathing more often than weekly was felt to be eccentric, besides wasn't good for one's health, might even bring on consumption. Doubtless, there was some rationalization in this, for pumping or drawing water, heating it, filling the tub, then emptying the bath water was a burdensome chore, and drafty rooms further discouraged the ritual. Etiquette writers felt the need to prod by associating personal cleanliness with inward purity, but most were vague as to just what extent bathing should be carried. One writer of the 1870s sought to set a minimum by adjuring that "just washing the eyes" was insufficient. Mrs. Mary Baker Eddy, on the other hand, attempted to set a maximum. "Cleanliness is next to godliness," she advised her faithful following, "but washing should be only to keep the body clean, and this can be done with less than daily scrubbing the whole surface."

However, with the advent of hot air furnaces, hot tap water, and tubs that drained themselves, the pleasure of frequent, lazy bathing was discovered as a sensual pleasure to be enjoyed for its own sake, perhaps just as Mrs. Eddy had feared. And no doubt patresfamilias reasoned that since they had spent all that money for expensive plumbing, it ought to be utilized, and so decreed. At any rate, the habit of regular bathing was accepted with almost revolutionary speed by those who could afford it, together with the habit of regularly changing one's underwear.

School teachers helped spread the new vogue for hygiene among the working classes, who, lacking bathtubs of their own, created a demand that revived the institution of the public baths, establishments especially for bathing purposes, forgotten since the Romans. In the 1890s, in Oakland and along the shoreline of Alameda's West End, the working boy or girl for five cents at a public bath house could acquire towel, soap, and ample hot water and get as clean as the rich. Martin Eden was quick to perceive that if he were to rise in the world he would need to wash frequently; he also invested in a toothbrush, an article he had never owned before. Cleanliness, it was discovered, was not merely next to Godliness, but one rung up toward gentility.

While Jack London was gazing from the outside in at all this magnificent altitude of living, taking his notes for future literary reference, another embryo Oakland writer was taking *hers* while gazing from the inside out. After an extended residence at the fashionable Tubbs Hotel, the Stein family moved into a big balustraded, wide-verandahed residence in East Oakland. Here Gertrude Stein spent her most impressionable years, and she always thought of it and Oakland as home, and with warm and lasting affection, even if she did once in a captious moment complain of Oakland, "There is no there there."

A rambling frame of mixed Victorian design, the Stein house was set on a slight rise from which sloped ten acres of eucalyptus and gum trees and fruit orchards; surrounding the house were butterfly-swept flower beds and winding walks, around which curved a Gothic picket fence. A neighbor's most vivid memory of the Stein place was that its fence was always glowing with red roses. In his opinion the lush beauty of the roses and of the flower garden accounted for Gertrude's luxuriant literary style. Robert Stewart some years ago was thus quoted in the Oakland *Tribune*: "She had been raised in a little coal mining town, and possibly the only flower she saw was a shriveled geranium in a pot on the window sill. So when she came to Oakland and found herself in the midst of a beautiful garden surrounded by a rose-covered fence, her deep nature was overwhelmed with the indescribable beauty . . . Her tongue went mute . . . Gertrude Stein could find no words adequate to convey the wonder that engulfed her and could only murmur . . . 'A rose is a rose is a rose.'" Actually Gertrude's experience hadn't been so lean as that. Her financier father had taken the family for a year's sojourn in Europe before moving them from Pennsylvania to Oakland, where he invested in an Oakland street railroad.

But certainly the little girl that another neighbor remembered for her "apple cheeks" and her "black hair in tightly-braided pigtails" stored up impressions quite unlike those assembled by Jack London. Long after she had established her famous literary salon in Paris, at which she, shingle-headed and tennis-shoed, enthralled the likes of Picasso and Hemingway, she wrote a book of memoirs in which she thus recalled her Oakland home: "It was wonderful there in the summer with the dry heat and the sun burning and the hot earth for sleeping; and then in the winter

This was the Lounging Room of Hotel Oakland during its heyday, when it hosted three United States Presidents: Woodrow Wilson, Calvin Coolidge, and Herbert Hoover. Other famous guests included Sarah Bernhardt, Amelia Earhart, and Charles Lindbergh. Designer of both the interiors and the building was the architectural firm of Bliss and Faville. The hotel's opening on December 23, 1912 was celebrated with a gala dinner attended by notables from all over California. Its aging elegance passed into wartime austerity in 1943, when the building was converted into a Veterans Administration hospital. Since the hospital closed its doors in 1964, the building has been vacant except for occasional use, but rumors of re-opening it or selling it persist. *(Albert Norman collection)*

with the rain and the north wind blowing that would bend the trees. Often break them, and the owls in the walls scaring you . . ." She remembered the eucalyptus trees as "so tall and thin and savage and the animals very wild." While revealing her deep involvement, her memories of Oakland always had a disquieting tone about them. She never mentioned roses in connection with Oakland.

If later a spectacular presence, in her Oakland days Gertrude blended quite harmoniously into proper blue serge Victorianism. She and her sister Julia paid decorous social calls with their mother. They stood for fittings with the family seamstress. She and her favorite brother Leo read the family volumes of *Pilgrim's Progress*, Sir Walter Scott, and Shakespeare, and spent their allowances on copies of Wordsworth and Shelley, designed their own bookplate and had it printed. They studied under a series of governesses, later attended a school at which Edwin Markham was headmaster. They played with neighbor children, who included Isadora and Raymond Duncan. In one of her books Gertrude accused Raymond (who by then in fringed toga was a familiar figure along the Champs Elysées) of having stolen apples from the Stein orchard.

Gertrude even possessed a typical Victorian father, whom she and her brothers and sisters dutifully obeyed while smoldering resentment. After the death of the mother, who had been a buffer, the estrangement widened. Of him she would write: "Fathers are depressing but our family had one." She described him as "not satisfied with anything," a "pounder of tables," a despot who decreed that Gertrude would be a musician, Leo a vinyardist, and their brother Simon a rancher. In this they would defy him. For, of course, Gertrude became Gertrude, Leo a dilettante expatriate, and Simon a gripman on a San Francisco cable car.

"It all went on," she recalled in her memoirs, "until one spring or summer. Then one morning we could not wake up our father. Leo climbed in by the window and called out to us that he was dead and he was." After claiming her share of the family fortune, Gertrude, already a purposeful young lady, departed for points East, carrying with her her Oakland-formed, highly-individual view of her planet.

125

Valentine-sending became a mania in the Victorian Era, perhaps because it permitted releasing all stops on sentiment. On February 14 throngs of messengers crisscrossed the city delivering dainty missives to palpitating recipients. Flower and bird designs were favorites, printed both on cards and on ingenious movable devices, such as the one at lower left that opens into a fan. Artistic types often preferred to confect their own Valentines from lace paper and paste-on figures that included a message such as "Dearly Beloved" or "Truly Thine." (North collection)

126

Geraniums, four-leaf clover, orange blossoms, and maiden-hair fern for Christmas? Yes, to Victorians such flowers and greenery were quite acceptable motifs for the Yule season. The geranium with parti-colored leaves pictured on card at upper left was an East Bay garden favorite. But holly with red berries was popular too, and both playful kittens and tranquil tabbies were universally popular designs, whether on a greeting card or a needlepoint pillow. *(North collection)*

Long the favorite place for a summer Sunday afternoon in Berkeley was the shady cool of Strawberry Canyon. There one might pick the luscious strawberries that gave the creek its name, or inspect the seedlings of the rare plants and trees that were being nurtured there for transplanting to the new University of California campus. Just a little way downstream at what is now Sather Gate, the crystal-clear water was spanned by a rustic footbridge wide enough for only one person.

(Berkeley Firefighters Association)

Pilgrims and Padres

It has been said that the height of exhilaration experienced by a prudish American upon acquiring a French mistress is excelled only by the heights of his contrition in the affair's aftermath. In the closing years of the Nineteenth Century, Americans began to feel as though they were at the end of a regrettable affair — their love affair, that is, with things European. With things voluptuous, gilded, ormolued, curvaceous, brocaded, garlanded; with things false-fronted, polished to too high a sheen; with things perfumed instead of scrubbed with honest soap and water.

Burgeoning national pride and power surely encouraged this attitude. So did dismay at the great emigrant tide from Europe — the "emigrant hordes" — which beat their way in such numbers to the servant's entrance. The cook, the gardener and the scullery maid were speaking European accents, while prompting the most hilarious anecdotes. "Have you heard what Bridget said to a caller yesterday?" Not to speak of outrageous servants' jokes. "Must you always spoil the meat?" "No mum, sometimes it comes bad from the butcher." And its variation: "Inga, is there *nothing* you can do right?" "Yes mum, I can milk reindeer." Somehow it had become less chic to boast, "Our house is Italian," or "That commode is Louis Quatorze." The cachet was gone, and eyes were glancing sidelong for something new.

The East repented first, donning the hair shirt of puritan dwellings — simple houses with rough-hewn shingles and beamed ceilings and high, crude fireplaces hung with cooking pots. At least, it started out that way. But archeology hadn't yet taught the nuances between Early American, Georgian, and Jefferson classic, and in the confusion all three were resuscitated in the name of Colonial. Given a sanctioned choice between a columned mansion and a slant-roofed salt box, most, naturally, opted for the former. Sometimes all three styles were commingled in one shingled, dormered, porticoed design. All three, of course, were really European, but purification had been achieved by association with our chaste ancestors.

The Bay Area with even more to repent of than the East, having so ardently embraced every style import, also began looking to its forebears. Observed the editor of a plan book published by Pacific States Savings, Loan and Building Company: "After our century of experiment, there is now a decided inclination to reproduce the same simple things that contented our grandfathers. We begin to realize that [they obtained] the maximum of elegance and convenience consistent with economy." One of his candidates for these maximums was a four-square, hip-roofed, gabled Georgian design that had the classic touch of elegant fluted Ionic pilasters set into the corners of the house. Enclosing ten rooms, it might be built for $10,000. The rectangular floor plan was back. After revels in the freedom of Gothic and Queen Anne's whimsical floor plans, it was decided that, after all, there was nothing so logical as a central hall with square rooms alongside.

Since one might identify with his ancestors with a baroque dwelling as easily as with a rustic one, the East Bay, like the Eastern Seaboard, most frequently chose elegance. Indeed, Colonial in the California sun tended to become a mansion, whether *grand ou petit*.

One local architect who readily shifted to Colonial was the Swiss-born architect William Mooser, who seems to have concocted his version of American Colonial while thumbing through old house plan books. He didn't hesitate to incorporate bay windows and king-size porches, wedding these to classic pilasters, Adams windows and French *oeil de boeuf* windows.

All these plus other embellishments were lavished on the house he built on Oakland's fashionable Jackson Street for Captain Thomas Mein, father of William Wallace Mein, Sr. It was a formidable white palace with a flight of gleaming marble steps leading to a mosaic-floored portico. Fan-lit doors admitted to a vestibule from which one entered a huge, round main hall flooded with magical light from a vast stained glass skylight. The arched ceiling was supported by an elegant peristyle of eight fluted columns. Around this color-splashed hall coiled and ascended a delicate circular staircase. The hall stairway and second story hall were wainscoted to a height of five feet with ornamented panels and all the doors were made to match.

This story-book house was built for a story-book character. Captain Mein already was well-known for his California mining ventures and for helping introduce hydraulic mining into California when, in 1892, he went prospecting in South Africa. There he quickly built up a fortune, supervising the Robinson Gold Mines, then the world's largest gold producer. The outbreak of the Boer War interrupted his career, and soon after he became an international cause célèbre when the Dutch sentenced him to death for high treason. The captain eventually was pardoned, but not before a harsh imprisonment had destroyed his health.

Returned to Oakland and grateful to be on home soil, the Captain yearned for a retreat that was one hundred per cent American and really felt he was getting it. Instead, his home would be derided by architecture scholars as a Colonial house totally devoid of Colonial spirit. The captain never heard these criticisms, however, for soon after moving in he died of the effects of his grueling ordeal. In 1920, the mansion became the first quarters for the new University Club of Alameda County, being christened with a speech by Earl Warren, then district attorney of Alameda County.

Not far from the Mein house, on Adams Street, stood another far from austere Colonial Revival, the "mainland" home of the wealthy Hawaiian plantation owner, Alexander Young, whose namesake hotel stands today in downtown Honolulu. The twenty-seven-room 1890 Young mansion, a combined classic-Georgian design, possessed such striking features as two decorative forty-foot chimneys and a great side portico supported by twelve majestic pillars of molded mortar. These deep colonnaded porticos, while rare in Eighteenth Century Colonial construction, were commonplace in Colonial Revival.

The Young mansion sold in 1910 to a buyer well able to maintain its tone, this being multimillionaire William Henshaw, who founded the old Union Savings Bank and erected the Henshaw Building in the Oakland commercial district. Mrs. Henshaw, who was one of the pretty daughters of early hotel man Hiram Tubbs, had gone to Vassar, later was presented at Court in London. It was their daughter Alla who made the aforementioned marriage with a Neopolitan prince to become the Princess Gion Capece Zurlo.

Adorning the shores of Lake Merritt was the classic house of John Russell Burnham, which had not one great columned portico but two, one square, the other half-moon-shaped. However, the Burnham home was best known for having the first shower stall in Oakland and an automobile garage. The Burnhams purchased one of the first two automobiles in town.

In Alameda, the architect B. E. Remmel designed for the F. W. Voogt family a rococo classic with a rather startling variety of windows, including three-tiered arched Palladian windows, round *oeil de boeuf* windows, rectangular windows with art glass, plain rectangular windows, and small

This one-story, high-perched version of Southern Colonial at 2040 Santa Clara Avenue in Alameda was sometimes called the Galveston Style, because the design evolved as a flood precaution. A utilitarian ground floor was concealed behind the wide front steps. Built by Jefferson Moser shortly after the 1906 earthquake, the house is the present-day abode of the Ham G. Lee family, who have retained the circular driveway, once used by carriages. (*Alameda Times Star*)

The real-life nineteenth century melodrama enacted in this Greek Revival mansion called Dunsmuir House was the subject of a motion picture. In 1962, the City of Oakland acquired the estate in the Oakland hills for use as a conference center. Many news-making seminars have since been held there, among them an international assembly of space scientists. *(City of Oakland)*

square windows. It had a half-circle front portico whose wide entrance steps led down one side to a swerving front walk.

More Puritan in spirit were the modest shingled cottages that were springing up in the East Bay, especially in Berkeley. One constructed in 1892 just south of the University of California campus for printing executive William E. Loy with its steep roof, second-story overhangs, and small-paned windows bore a striking resemblance to Paul Revere's house in Boston. Yet, this house too had no connection with the American Colo-

nies, other than that its architect Ernest Coxhead had recently arrived from England and, like the Pilgrims, had remembered the style of the rural English cottages. Coxhead had practiced briefly in Los Angeles before moving to San Francisco; later he would contribute to development of the Bay Area style.

Loy's daughter Eugenia married William E. Chamberlain, a nationally-known musician, and after they occupied the house in 1906 the large redwood-paneled living room was the scene of frequent gala concerts. Chamberlain helped found the San Francisco Opera, and many organizational meetings were held at the house. In 1968, when the house sold to a developer, it was the object of a spirited campaign by the Berkeley Art Commission which sought to preserve it as an architectural landmark, but financing failed and the dwelling was razed to make way for one more apartment building.

No doubt, our humble ancestors would have felt at home with the crude cedar shingles, the rough-hewn beamed ceiling and the simple pine wainscoting of the Baum's Colonial cottage in Alameda. But the dwelling bore certain non-rustic touches that inspired this comment from a correspondent for *Architect and Engineer of California:* "Among the picturesque homes overlooking the bay in Alameda probably none is more attractive than the palatial residence of Alexander Baum." Palatial, indeed, were such features as French windows opening onto terraces, decorative tile mantels, and an elegant winding staircase with a dais platform that overlooked the living room, reception hall, and dining room.

Another Colonial variation was Southern Colonial, actually styles favored in the Deep South during the early decades of the Nineteenth Century when plantation life was in its glory and cotton was king. Two Southern styles were revived in the Bay Area, both put together of classical components.

One was a squat design that at first glance appeared to be a high-perched one-story house. A long flight of broad entrance steps led to an encircling columned veranda almost concealing an entire under floor at ground level. This was the so-called Galveston Style, which had been popular all along the Gulf Coast in pre-seawall days when flooding was frequent. Jefferson Davis' home "Beauvoir" at Biloxi, Mississippi, was so styled. The function of the design, as in the river Victorians in Sacramento, was to lift the main floor out of reach of high water. The roof was without a pediment, which would have looked foolish on so flat a design; instead a classic dental cornice bordered a shallow hip roof.

High in the Piedmont hills where no flood ever lapped, not even primeval ones, was constructed a charming example of this style. Forty-niner Jesse

Probably the most popular remaining Mission Revival Style structure in the Bay Area is the serenely beautiful Bell Tower at Mills College in Oakland. The gift to the college of Mr. and Mrs. F. M. Smith, the tower was designed by Julia Morgan in 1904 as part of a group of buildings that included the college library, gymnasium, and social hall. The bells, ten in all, date from 1893 when they were cast in Cincinnati for the Columbian Exposition in Chicago; they also hung at San Francisco's Mid-winter Fair the following year. *(North collection)*

Lamereaux Wetmore, a native of New Brunswick, built it for his family on a site now bordered by the Piedmont City Hall. To the classic deep-verandahed design, Wetmore, who was an Oakland contractor, added incongruous touches of lacy millwork, probably through habit. Instead of classic columns, the veranda has turned posts and a balustrade; at the foot of the wide entrance steps are urn-shaped newel posts. The windows have mullioned glass.

Before he was an Oakland contractor Wetmore was a business partner of storied "Honest Harry" Meiggs of San Francisco wharf ventures. After

Benicia on the Carquinez Straits not only lost its original name, Francisca, to San Francisco, but lost its prime asset, the state capital, to Sacramento. For one proud year — 1853 to 1854 — the handsome Greek Revival building above with its fluted Doric columns served as the capitol of California. It is a well-preserved monument in present-day Benicia, along with St. Paul's Episcopal Church and the arsenal that includes a guardhouse that once held young Lt. Ulysses S. Grant. *(Bancroft Library)*

Built in 1854 in Martinez, this stone courthouse in the Greek Revival Style served until 1903. It was demolished after a new courthouse was erected on the site of the pictured water tower. The red brick addition at rear served as the county jail. *(Wells Fargo Bank History Room)*

"Honest Harry" was obliged to flee to South America in the wake of a financial scandal, Wetmore followed, and the partners prospered in South American railroad building. Wetmore's son Clarence was, of course, that young man famed in University of California annals for being its first registrant and a member of its first graduating class. And it was that historic first graduation day that drew Wetmore père back to Oakland, where he decided to remain and invest in the real estate boom.

The two Wetmore daughters, Ida and Anna, never married and lived in the house into advanced old age with their thirty-two cats. After their death, the then dilapidated house was nearly lost to the wrecking ball, but a public campaign stayed demolition until it could be purchased by an owner prepared to rehabilitate and preserve it. It has since been included in the federal government's Historic American Building Survey.

That other Southern Colonial was, of course, ante-bellum Greek Revival, or Classical-Colonial. As unlike as were the swampy flats of Louisiana and the Coast Range bordering San Francisco Bay, both provided settings for grand private Parthenons. And rivaling in beauty those moldering amidst the Louisiana bayous is one that was constructed in a broad-sweeping canyon in the Oakland hills and today glistens in almost pristine condition.

Dunsmuir House with its great, white Doric columns under a majestic, wide pointed pediment, has the look of a movie set — you can almost hear carriage wheels crunching in the drive. And, in fact, its story did inspire a melodramatic movie, *Alexander Dunsmuir's Dilemma,* whose real-life protagonist was as handsome as any leading man who auditioned for the role. Alexander Dunsmuir was fabulously rich as well, an heir to the huge Vancouver Island coal mining empire founded by his father Scotsman Robert Dunsmuir. He had seemed to have everything, but the silver spoon in his mouth quickly tarnished.

As a young man, "Alex" had shown more interest in amour than in business, and his mother, aware of his weakness, strongly opposed his being sent as the firm's representative to San Francisco, a city she had heard was "fast." The father nonsensed this, and in 1878 Alex arrived in San Francisco, where his actions could scarcely have been better calculated to distress his pious mother.

By night, a svelte figure with red-tinged sideburns, he haunted the gayest theaters. At one of them he became the crony of the head usher, an agreeable young man named Waller Wallace. Invited to the Wallace home, Alex promptly became taken with Wally's wife, Josephine, a petite brunette who had grown up on a farm behind Oakland and was said to have been as fetching as a Dresden shepherdess. Before long Alex was installed as a lodger in the Wallace household, from which soon after Wally precipitously exited, taking the couple's small son and daughter with him.

However, the complicating third point of the triangle proved not to be Wally, who capitulated rather docilely (at Alex' insistence, he even returned the little girl to her mother); instead it was Alex' stern and powerful mother who inflexibly decreed from her Craigdarroch Castle in Victoria that her son would marry "that adventuress" at the price of being disinherited. In short, the third point of the triangle was money. Alex found himself immobilized by his plight: on one side was Josephine pleading for him to give her respectability by making her Mrs. Dunsmuir; on the other was his desire to keep his fortune. Unable to resolve this dilemma, he took to drink.

Years passed, a decade slipped by, with no break in the stalemate. Alex' father died, but his mother remained unrelenting toward Josephine, nor did she relax her control over the family business. The only change was that Alex accelerated his drinking and Josephine's health began to decline. Her one pleasure was the vicarious one she took in the success of her daughter; her little girl had grown up to be a beautiful stage actress and had married the popular comedian DeWolf Hopper. Billed as Edna Wallace Hopper, she was the toast of Broadway.

Finally, in desperation Alex (by then in his forties, as was his faded paramour) entered into a secret pact with his brother James, a kick-back arrangement financially advantageous to the latter providing he coaxed the mother into making a division. It was after making this pact that Alex, in 1897, acquired the Oakland property, the site of the farm where Josephine had grown up, and engaged the architect Eugene Freeman to build

135

Colonial Revival houses, characterized by Palladian detailing at windows and cornice and by columned porticos, were praised for their symmetry and good proportion. The style was more popular in the East Bay than in San Francisco. Formerly the Worden residence, this pleasant house at 418 Thirtieth Street in Oakland now houses doctors' offices. *(Oakland Public Library)*

Classic wasn't confined to mansions and public buildings. This miniature Greek temple, carefully correct with its Ionic columns, pilasters, entablature, pediment, and crowning balustrade, accommodated the practice of an Alameda dentist around the turn of the century. *(Alameda Historical Society)*

136

a splendid mansion for the woman who had waited two decades to be his wife.

No expense was spared in constructing the grand house, or the private waterworks and electric light plant, or on the grounds landscaped with rare exotics and tropical foliage and graced with a spectacular electric waterfall. The house was completed with still no change in Victoria, but Alex moved Josephine in anyway and had it inserted in an Oakland gossip column that they had been secretly wed for years.

Even with an alliance against her, the mother held out until December, 1899, when she was finally pressured into selling her interest in the firm, while still calling wrath upon the woman she felt had bewitched her son. James relayed the news to Oakland, where Alex and Josephine made arrangements to be married clandestinely, in keeping with the nurtured illusion that they were long-married.

A family friend fetched a minister to perform the ceremony, but having heard of Alex' advanced alcoholism, the minister insisted upon first interviewing the forty-six-year-old bridegroom to ascertain his competence. At last the vows were exchanged in a hotel room in San Pablo, and soon after the couple boarded a train for a "business trip" to New York that was really their honeymoon. That is if it can be called a honeymoon with the groom most of the journey in his berth steeped in alcohol and his bride in hers weak from the mortal illness she was suffering.

In New York Josephine's sole happiness was in being reunited with Edna, who was opening in a new play. Her groom's days were spent partly in delirium, partly in coma; he died there of alcoholic dementia just forty days after his wedding. Josephine then pinned her hopes on the surgical operation she hoped would save her life. It was unsuccessful, as was a second, and she died the following year, leaving the wedding gift house to Edna who, in process of divorcing DeWolf Hopper, put it up for sale. It passed through a succession of owners before it was acquired by the City of Oakland as a municipal conference center. Today this legendary house is the setting of solemn seminars on taxes and dock improvements.

James Leonard, one of the four Americans who settled Berkeley, in his old age set himself up in shining splendor in a partially Greek Revival man-

A vision of colonial splendor was the John Hind mansion with its sweeping terraced lawn. The Hawaiian plantation owner came to Berkeley to establish a home at the turn of the century to give his two daughters an American education. The house, which stood at 208 The Uplands, be- came the nucleus of the Claremont Park district after it was developed by Mason-McDuffie. The brown shingled and gabled house across the road is the Rosenthal home, which still stands. The Hind house was demolished in the late 1930s. (*Albert Norman collection*)

Berkeley's redwood shingles adapted readily to the Georgian style. This well-preserved shingle house at 2446 Prospect Street that dates from 1904 is the home of Myron Leenhouts. With its shuttered small-paned windows and pedimented entrance, it might well stand on a street in Colonial Williamsburg, Virginia — that is if its exterior material were brick or horizontal boards. While the Georgian style was derived from the Italian architect Palladio, it was much used and modified in England during the reign of the four Georges. (T. W. Tenney)

sion on Telegraph Avenue. The long rectangular house, with an eight-columned veranda that set into the rectangle instead of extending from it, was centered on frontage that stretched the entire block between Russell and Oregon Streets. Above the veranda three incongruous dormers protruded from the roof. The interior glistened with golden oak paneling and a golden oak staircase that was gloriously illumined from its landing by a great three-tiered stained-glass window.

Leonard could well afford his showplace, thanks to a lucky draw in 1852. After he, Frank Shattuck, George Blake, and William Hillegass claimed a square mile of land in the heart of what was to become central Berkeley under the newly-enacted Possessory Rights Law, they drew straws to see which quarter each would get. Leonard drew the straw for the southeast corner, a district which would skyrocket in value with the opening of the University two decades later.

Despite these spectacular examples, Greek Revival never really caught on in the Bay Area. To be successful it required a client of the financial caliber of a Dunsmuir, or Leonard, or of a J. T. Barraclough, whose temple-like residence rose imperiously on his Piedmont Olympus on Hillside Avenue. Nor did any Colonial style cut a really sizable swath locally (except in public buildings and schools, such as the Oakland Technical High School); California architects never really warmed up to it, feeling it didn't harmonize with the native terrain. Besides, they were tired of following suit.

Berkeley poet and architecture critic Charles Keeler spoke for the profession when he proclaimed in print: "With the California houses which pass under the name of 'Colonial' I have no sympathy whatever." He scoffed at the "meaningless white-painted fluted columns of hollow wood, which support nothing worthy of their pretentiousness" and felt the "little balconies of turned posts, which are too small or inaccessible to be used" to be ridiculously incongruous when set down amidst the glare of the Pacific slope. He expressed particular pain at one large East Bay Georgian house painted red to hint of brick and trimmed with white painted frame that pretended to be granite.

138

In the nimble nineties came the bicycles, wheeling democratically even up into the aristocratic Piedmont hills. Cycling was a fad of major proportions, with men and women alike joining one or more clubs. Some clubs preferred the high-wheeled bicycle pictured below, although it frightened the horses even more than the conventional variety. A bicycling club in proper masculine bicycling attire poses for a portrait before the Isaac Requa mansion. The feminine bicycling costume included fitted bolero, leg-o-mutton sleeves and a divided skirt. *(Albert Norman collection)*

But if Colonial was in order, it occurred to someone (precisely *who* is lost to history), then why not California Colonial? Why not build in the style the Spanish padres built their missions? Most likely the idea was prompted by the mission preservation movement which had gotten under way in 1884, in Carmel, setting an example that inspired the later restoration of Mission Dolores in San Francisco. After decades of trying to obliterate all traces of the vanquished Spaniard, Californians suddenly had awakened romantically to their Spanish heritage. They were staging colorful costume parades called "Pageants of Romantic California" and were restoring adobes as zealously as they formerly had desecrated them (restoring too elegantly, alas; most early restorations have had to be restored again in the interests of authenticity).

The idea caught on, and a call went up for a "genuine native architecture," for "buildings suited to our locale." One architect was thus quoted: "Give me neither Romanesque nor Gothic, much less Italian Renaissance, and least of all English Colonial. This is California — give me Mission!" Didn't the California climate, it was reasoned, require a different kind of architecture from that of the Eastern Seaboard?

While many agreed that it did, Mission might never have risen from the rubble had not a young St. Louis architect arrived to spur the resurrection. Ebullient Willis Polk, a descendant of James K. Polk, came to San Francisco, after working under Daniel Burnham in Chicago. He took a job as an assistant to architect A. Page Brown and not only caught the Mission fever but confidently seized its standard. His rustic retreat

The simple, dignified red brick building, above, with the tile roof was the Berkeley Public Library from 1905 until 1929, when it was razed to make way for the present main library at Shattuck and Kittredge. Berkeley received the library as a gift. Andrew Carnegie donated the $40,000 building; Rosa M. Shattuck gave the land. *(Berkeley Fire-fighters Association)*

The Piedmont home, below, of the realtor and street car magnate Frank C. Havens was surrounded by a dry garden — a sort of reverse terrarium — in which grew hearty, fibrous plants native to the American desert and to South Africa. The Havens later built their Indian-style home, Wildwoods, on the garden site. *(Albert Norman collection)*

This handsomely patterned brick sheathing and molded terra cotta grace a vintage commercial building at 2069 Addison Street that in one way or another is familiar to nearly all Berkeleyans. It housed the pioneer Golden Sheaf Bakery, first operated by John Wright, which served the growing town for decades. Horse-drawn wagons loaded with fragrant fresh-baked bread, cakes and pies delivered Golden Sheaf products door to door uphill and down, also taking orders for the next day. Later, when telephones came in, housewives phoned in their day's bakery needs. The building, just a few steps off Shattuck Avenue, now stands vacant except for the ground-floor level that now provides parking for a men's clothing shop. (*T. W. Tenney*)

Berkeley's most splendid Mission Revival house was built by Klondike prospector and oil magnate Howard Hart on Alvarado Road. Note its use of the star window, copied from Mission San Carlos Borromeo at Carmel. Hart lavished $700,000 on the house with its forty-three rooms filled with murals, paintings, statuary, and other mementos of the Harts' extensive world travels. *(Louis Stein collection)*

Succeeding the Mission Revival style by a decade was Spanish Revival, which was more Mediterranean than Franciscan. The house below, at 2957 Avalon Avenue in Berkeley, presently the home of Dr. George Lenczowski, has a charming secluded patio behind the adobe wall. *(Berkeley Daily Gazette)*

"Stagden" in the Oakland hills became a gathering place for Mission buffs, among them Ernest Coxhead. Together they speculated with sketch pads how the simple motif might be made to serve contemporary needs. They tramped on week-end archeological hunts, often finding picturesque Spanish ruins given over to cattle barns and chicken runs. In San Pablo, however, they found an ancient Spanish structure that somehow had defied weather and wanton destruction, an 1837 adobe that had housed Spanish official functions. (Today it is revered as the oldest house in the Bay Region.)

In 1890, Polk got the grandiose inspiration of spreading the Mission word with a new magazine. *Architecture News* appeared in November, its elegant parchment-like pages devoted to writings and drawings of mission architecture, old, new and imagined. After three issues the restless Polk gave it up and hied to Carmel (with the subscription money, it is said). But by then he had launched Mission Revival.

And so along the East Bay's curving avenues appeared a new contender: houses with low, almost windowless plaster walls with protruding beams, with simple arched doorways and roofs of bright red terra cotta tile. The plaster was roughly dashed to simulate adobe; the bareness was dramatically accented with cast iron window grills, door bracketry, and wall lanterns. Of course, neither the size nor shape of these houses bore any resemblance to the elongated arcaded monastic chapels and dormitories for accommodating monks and Indians. But their purposes bore no resemblance either, and captious observers were quick to note that the style did not satisfactorily serve the family unit which engaged in more specialized tasks than shelling corn and tanning hides; the shadowy interiors were criticized for their lack of light.

Still, these houses with their white slab sides crowned with dazzling red roofs were quite prepossessing, especially when designed by architects of the sensitivity of Willis Polk. They were infinitely more tasteful than the hoked-up Hollywood-style Spanish of the 1920s. Polk's work became more authentic during the course of his painstaking restoration of Mission Dolores, for which he studied tile-making and the Franciscan method of wood framing.

A less perceptive architect attempted the impossible in seeking to translate the style of the vast mission complex into a low-cost cottage. *California Architect and Building News* published a model of a Mission Cottage designed by John Knapp to sell at $1,500. A cube of whitewashed stucco with meager plaster-and-lath arches and a band of imitation tile, it was the epitome of skimpiness. But that didn't prevent its being copied all around the Bay.

The most famous Mission Revival house in the East Bay, leaving all contenders trailing behind, was the residence of Mrs. Phoebe Hearst, the mother of publisher William Randolph Hearst. It crowned a green knoll overlooking fields and vineyards near Pleasanton, and its name was Hacienda del Pozo de Verona, derived from the romantic marble fountain in its patio, brought from the ancient city where Romeo and Juliet are supposed to have lived.

Ironwork and Victorian gingerbread go together like a horse and carriage. The inspiration for the lacy designs was Gothic tracery. This lyrical fence still complements an early frame house in west Berkeley. (*T. W. Tenney*)

143

Hacienda del Pozo de Verona was the name that Mrs. Phoebe Hearst gave to her Spanish-style house in the Livermore hills, but it was popularly known as "The Hacienda." Filled with rare art treasures, it was the scene of highly original entertaining. When the guest list was sizable, Mrs. Hearst provided a special railroad car for transportation from Oakland to her private railroad station at Verona. The Oakland society columnist Roxie thus de-

scribed the arrival of guests for an all-day Fourth of July fete: "At Verona Station carriages awaited the guests, and the large procession winded its way up the hillside . . . suddenly you are driven through the courtyard and you forget everything else, for there in the doorway is Mrs. Hearst, the same gracious hostess as of old." (*William Apperson collection*)

Mrs. Hearst built it after being widowed by George Hearst, the mining prospector and United States Senator who was twenty-two years her senior, and she presided over the Hacienda and its endless procession of distinguished guests as a woman famous in her own right as a philanthropist and patroness of the arts.

She returned to California in the late-1890s after extensive art-collecting travels in Europe with the plan of building a showcase for her treasures on family property in the Livermore Valley. Some years before her son "Willie" had had the architect A. C. Schweinfurth build a hunting lodge there, and now to enlarge and transform it into her dream, Mrs. Hearst brought in the young Oakland-born architect Julia Morgan, who had recently graduated from the École des Beaux-Arts and was working in the office of John Galen Howard, architect for the University of California.

Mrs. Hearst was less influenced by the revival of Mission than she was by her enthusiasm for Spanish architecture she had admired abroad.

The design she and Miss Morgan arrived at was a blend that combined the Mission style with Hispano-Moresque. This felicitous meeting of minds — the beginning of a long succession of Hearst-Morgan collaborations — created an arresting silhouette against the blue valley sky: a pair of great, square towers soaring over a cluster of red tile roofs, the whole encompassed by a massive wall with parapets. When approaching through the tower-flanked main gates, the eye was drawn to vine-wrapped pergolas, decorative grilled windows, serene balconies, and, at ground level, inviting courts and arcades shaded with climbing jasmine and rose. To landscape her Hacienda and its multiple courts, Mrs. Hearst had engaged the famed botanist, Luther Burbank.

Inside, Mrs. Hearst and her guests revolved between the various summer apartments and the sumptuous winter suite furnished with Renaissance cabinets, Gothic credences, rare tapestries, a handsome Louis XVI clock, portraits by Romney and Gainsborough, Della Robbia reliefs, two Corots and a Millet. The music room was de-

144

scribed as being "elaborately carved, gilded, and enameled in designs peculiar to the period in which Spanish art was informed by Moorish influence."

Her hospitality was lavish, while taking an intellectual tone. The guest list frequently included University notables, for already she was probing how she might best assist the University, which soon would become her prime philanthropic project. Among her much-talked-of entertainments was a dinner honoring a famous Egyptologist who had just returned from a University of California-sponsored archeological expedition that she had financed. For the occasion, the patio around the famous fountain was transformed into an Egyptian setting with full-sized palm trees, hanging fern, lotus blossoms, vast candelabras, and a high blue canopy studded with tiny electric lights that simulated the constellations in the Egyptian night sky. Attendants in Egyptian costume served the guests, who were presented souvenir cartouche rings and Eye of Horus amulets, all this to a background concert of the orchestral music from Verdi's *Aida*.

After Mrs. Hearst died in 1919, her son, by then the world-famous publisher of the Hearst chain of newspapers, had the fountain of Verona moved to San Simeon, his castle on the Pacific that Julia Morgan was designing for him. He sold the Hacienda to a group that founded the Castlewood Country Club. Late one Sunday night in 1969, fire broke out in one of the parapets, quickly putting club members to flight. Firemen, hampered by a lack of hydrants, pumped the famous Olympic-size swimming pool almost dry, but were no match for the engulfing flames that left only two tall chimneys and blackened stucco walls.

Another admired semi-Spanish design was the Piedmont mansion of William E. Sharon, namesake nephew of the former Alamedan who became Nevada's flamboyant "Bonanza Senator" and object of a sensational suit by a woman who claimed to be his secret wife. The younger Sharon, known to his friends as "Billy," while superintending his uncle's interests in the Comstock, had married a beautiful Virginia City belle. Their first home in Oakland was in the Lake Merritt district, but the highly social Mrs. Sharon found her hostessing talents somewhat circumscribed at

that address, and her admiring husband built the Piedmont house to give her accomplishments full scope.

It proved one of the most popular sights and social meccas of the East Bay. Situated on a rise on lofty Mountain Avenue, the house had two great square minaret-like towers, one at either end of the long, rectangular design. And like the new Spanish buildings at Stanford University, it incorporated Romanesque details; at the center of the long facade fanned a great ornamental arch, such as those employed by the Chicago architect Louis Sullivan.

Mrs. Sharon christened her elegant new home with a far from simple afternoon tea. Friends responding to formal engraved invitations arrived to find the guest of honor to be the world-famous opera singer Madame Emma Nevada. The stunning blonde prima donna, a gorgeous gown hugging her generous curves, smilingly greeted the enthralled guests while an orchestra throbbed in the background. Then, at a long table glittering with silver and cut glass, a delightful new tea custom was introduced to the Bay Area. A uniformed maid quietly inquired of each guest, "Do you wish rum in the tea?" For those with enough aplomb to conceal surprise and murmur yes, Mrs. Sharon dribbled into their cups a few drops of rum from a most decorous jug. This culinary innovation was said to have been imported from the London drawing room of Senator Sharon's daughter, Lady Hesketh.

Mission practitioners not only engaged in style-mixing, as in the Sharon house, but freely substituted materials, sometimes employing something so uncharacteristic as irregular fieldstone set in mortar. And while one might suppose that here, surely, was a style that resisted wood, one would be dead wrong. Mission Revival houses were indeed constructed of wood.

The afore-mentioned plan book published by Pacific States Savings, Loan & Building Company included a Mission house designed for construction at $9,000 for which wood was the designated building material. Extending the entire length of the wide first floor was a combination terrace-veranda with a ripple of wide arches, simulating the old mission arcades. But the second floor with its overhangs and perpendicular woodwork trim

The multiple arches ranged at ground level in this elongated design by Julia Morgan suggest the arcade of a Franciscan mission. It was the main building of Miss Ransome and Miss Bridges' School on Piedmont's Hazel Lane, providing both dormitory rooms and classrooms for the exclusive private school for girls that attracted students from all over the country and from Central and South America. *(North collection)*

was really more Swiss chalet than Mission, while extending from one side was a porte-cochère. The plan book lauded the design's "practical simplicity and peaceful domestic air." It also observed that the design was "entirely distinct from ecclesiastic expression," which it indubitably was.

Mission became California's second architectural export. However, the architect who succeeded in introducing Mission Revival to the nation wasn't Polk, but his employer whom he had helped to convert, A. Page Brown. Brown's Mission style entry in the competition for the California Building at the Columbian Exposition in Chicago came off winner. Mission was, of course, readily adaptable to a building of the scale of the Fair building, and Brown's much-admired design precipitated a rash of adaptations all over the country. More than two decades later California chose the Mission style for its own world fair, the Panama-Pacific International Exposition of 1915. The California Building, the design of T. H. F. Burditt, was a gigantic and rather cluttered composite of motifs from several of the Franciscan missions.

An off-shoot of Mission was the Mediterranean Style, or rather, a revival of the various styles of the Mediterranean Coast. This came about when architects began to encounter difficulties fitting an ecclesiastical architecture to modern needs and sought reasonable facsimiles. The architect Bert Croly argued that the Mediterranean Style was the logical design for Riviera-like California, and claimed it was what the padres were really aiming for. Willis Polk built some charming East Bay residences in the Italian Mediterranean Style, including one in Berkeley for Duncan McDuffie.

As serenely attuned to its urban setting today as the day it was built is the home of Mrs. Selden Williams at 2821 Claremont Boulevard in Berkeley. It was designed by Julia Morgan, one of the foremost practitioners of the Mediterranean Style, the echo of Mission Revival, that transformed much of California's landscape during the 1920s. The building specifications repeatedly called for the work to be done "in an absolutely first class manner." The contractor was D. B. Farquharson. (*Berkeley Daily Gazette*)

But the most popular Mediterranean Style of the late Victorian Era was the so-called Morisco, or Moorish style, doubtless because it indulged the Victorian's die-hard craving for the ornate. Much admired was the Alameda mansion of Colonel A. H. Ward on elegant South Paru Street, which was named *Gracias-a-dios*. The design of architect Fuller Chaflin, it boasted two Byzantine domes, one at either end of the flat-roofed, rectangular structure. A froth of ornamented Moorish arches on the facade recalled the Alhambra Palace in Granada, and in spirit the Alhambra Palace is, of course, light years away from the simple Franciscan Mission.

Unlike Queen Anne, Mission had proved unaccommodating. All the departures and substitutions and shortcuts had turned it into quite something else. But by that time, even its most ardent early proponents, Polk among them, realized their error in trying to adapt to modern use the primitive architecture of a religious order, construction that was fitted to simple needs and to an open situation. The mission's long horizontal lines simply didn't fit urban building sites, while its blank walls were against the trend for sunlit rooms. Too late they saw that their striving could only have resulted in debasement of form and falsification of materials.

Victorians had looked to their forebears for architectural inspiration, and their forebears had led them frivolously astray. Colonial had merely opened a side door back into tired and debased classicism, while Mission in its stubborn refusal to adapt had proven a dead-end street.

147

While April 18, 1906, was by no means run-of-the-mill in the East Bay, citizens counted their blessings over escaping San Francisco's fate. Earthquake damage was relatively minor — this building on Broadway was among the worst hit — and the Oakland *Tribune* could make this reassuring report: "Oakland, Berkeley and Alameda have suffered no material damage. Our shops and transportation agencies are unimpaired and ready for immediate use." The East Bay welcomed more than 200,000 refugees from across the Bay, setting up camps in parks and churches, and taking many into private homes. Such was East Bay hospitality, more than a third remained as permanent residents. (*Albert Norman collection*)

Shingles on the Hillside

The failure of Mission Revival didn't dampen the ardor for architectural change. For change hovered in the air along with great expectations. The last decade of the Nineteenth Century was popularly known as *fin de siècle,* and with the new century approaching everybody was feeling on the brink. But of *what?* Nobody knew for certain. As the San Franciscan Amelia Neville recalled in her delightful memoirs *The Fantastic City:* "It was the fashion to be 'end of century' in everything — which meant to be modernistic with an added flash of the bizarre." Which meant, that is, to be daringly different from what had gone before.

Of course, everybody assumed that the upcoming century would be simply fabulous, but with no reliable clues to go on as just how to prepare for it, then the only thing to do was to reverse everything. Thus whatever was iconoclastic or revolutionary was thought to be very *fin de siècle.* Such as Aubrey Beardsley's irately irreverent drawings, and Ambrose Bierce's ripping satires on everything in sight. Such as the eccentric Art Nouveau and double-entendre songs. Bicycles and culottes to wear astride them. And a tortured hair-do called the "automobile tousel," even though few automobiles were abroad yet.

All before had been all wrong, or so it seemed. Houses, especially. Even the cozy, inviting Victorian kitchen had been wrong. It had been much too crowded, cluttered, and inconvenient. What was wanted was a "workshop." The new magazine for Western women *Home Chimes* ("Published in beautiful Berkeley . . . to introduce into every household a chord of harmony") explained how the kitchen might be converted into an airy "housewife's workshop" by storing kitchen equipment and supplies on shelves sunk beneath the floor. The housewife commanded the shelf to ascend into the uncluttered air by pressing her foot upon a "mysterious lever." When she had claimed what she needed, down went the shelf again.

Some advanced thinkers were for moving the kitchen upstairs. In the past half century, upper-class kitchens had progressed from basement to first floor, and now some felt they should be lifted to the top floor to permit cooking odors and vapors to escape without filtering offensively through living quarters. The *California Architect and Building News* of March, 1893, endorsed this much-discussed move, observing: "Ill-smelling fumes from saucepan, pot and kettle diffuse their volume in parlor, hall, and chambers . . . The preparation of salted codfish and mackerel is long known to the nose before those eatables greet the sight." Anticipating that transporting fuel and supplies to the upstairs kitchen might present a

149

French furniture in the patio? Yes, and carpeting, too. It was part of the breezy *fin de siècle* life style. To live outdoors as much as possible was considered healthful, while *al fresco* entertaining was the height of chic. Thus, an outdoor living room was practically a necessity. Of course, the problem of air pollution was decades away. (*Bancroft Library*)

problem, the writer suggested a "properly planned and constructed dumb-waiter." He recommended that the dining room also be placed in the upper region.

The parlor likewise came under attack. First, its name was discarded as tacky. During the *fin de siècle* years it came to be known as the library (an ephemeral label, it turned out, for decorators were soon to arrive at "living room.") To justify the new term a bookcase was usually moved in, but some rooms were libraries by virtue of having a few magazines scattered about.

But the big news with parlors — libraries, rather — was that quaintness had given way to the new sought-after trio of simplicity, naturalness, and casualness. Virtue now lay in "avoiding everything tending to display." Overstuffed chairs and sofas were passé. The thing to have was Mission furniture, those starkly plain, straight, square, all-wood pieces that sometimes had leather cushions, sometimes were as hard as a church pew.

Mission furniture, like Mission architecture, had evolved in California from Franciscan inspiration, and was the region's first contribution to furniture design. This progenitor of today's functional furniture looked as if it were made of house timbers, and sometimes was. Indeed, much of it was hammered together by house carpenters, and according to *California Architect and Engineer* "Many a man who has built his own house has been able to construct his furniture as well from these models, patience being the main tool used in its making along with careful measurements and well-seasoned wood."

150

Home Chimes decreed that the "successful home . . . must look simple" — quite a revolutionary notion for the Victorian Era. "It must seem easy to keep in order and just enough in order to prove it is not neglected" was their tantalizingly vague advice. The editors strongly urged homemakers to jettison their carpets and make do with bare floors regularly scrubbed with borax, thus serving not only simplicity but also hygiene, which was very in too. If one must have floor coverings, then settle for rag rugs you could wash, or straw mats you could shake. Drapes were scorned as well; all that was wanted were simple burlap curtains which freely admitted the breeze that was blowing through the newly opened windows.

Instead of dusting fussy curios and objets d'art, suggested the editors, why not cultivate house plants such as fern or palms. Berkeley's Charles Keeler writing in his popular book *The Simple Home* likewise urged rusticity. He suggested as a substitute for "showy vases" the display of such unpretentious objects as earthenware pots, wine flasks, bellows, and baskets, "especially those of our own misused Indians." Instead of wallpaper, he recommended natural planed red-wood walls, or rough boards left unpainted and colored with a green creosote stain to lend a mossy effect.

Simplicity also stamped the dining room, until recently smothered with red velvet curtains, floor-sweeping lace tablecloths, and Oriental rugs. *Home Chimes* suggested buying unfinished tables and chairs from the factory, painting them white along with the woodwork. All of this was to be washed and dried every week or ten days. "Think how clean it all is," trilled the author, who recommended as cover for the table a brief scarf of plain denim.

These bare, sterile interiors catered to the new regimen of courting health with pure, fresh air, indoors as well as out. Indoors, one lived in breeze-swept rooms, and at night, if one was available, slept on a screened sleeping porch. Both sexes contrived to stay outdoors as much as possible in pursuit of sports — badminton, tennis, cycling, sailing, and hiking in the hills. On fete days, to benefit charity, the grounds of the larger estates were thrown open to East Bay society, whose members competed vigorously with each other on the athletic courts and then paused, flush-faced, to sip tea in a gazebo. The new sports-lov-

The vogue for ostrich feathers made Oakland one of the centers for ostrich raising during the years 1904 to 1917. Ladies were eager to pay $10 to $15 each for fine feathers with which to bedeck themselves or to set off a jardinière on a newel post. A full-grown bird yielded four hundred of the colorful plumes, while supplying four-pound eggs that sold at $3 each for souvenirs (note egg hamper on salesroom floor). The profitable birds, imported from South Africa, obligingly thrived on a modest diet of grass, grain and gravel. At the intersection of Fourteenth and High Streets, there stood an ostrich farm salesroom on each corner, one the outlet for the Golden State Ostrich Farm. The herds roamed behind the salesrooms, and consisted sometimes of as many as fifty of the fluffy nine-foot creatures. The enclosure fences were extraordinarily stout, since a single kick from one of the high-tempered, muscular birds could splinter an ordinary fence post.
(Albert Norman collection)

151

SALESROOM AND OFFICE
GOLDEN STATE OSTRICH FARM
EAST 14TH AND HIGH STREETS
OAKLAND, CALIFORNIA

On a September day in 1901, Berkeley firemen posed solemnly before their firehouse that is draped in mourning for President William McKinley. The martyred President, felled by an anarchist's bullet in Buffalo, had visited the East Bay only the previous June. At that time he addressed a large East Bay gathering at the corner of Oakland's Lake and Oak Streets, making a speech, which according to one news account "was so informal that each one felt as though he had had a personal interview with the President, whose manners were graciousness itself." (*Berkeley Firefighters Association*)

ing, shirtwaisted woman cultivated these new interiors as appropriate to her new image, just as her languid, sun-eschewing counterpart of a decade before had reveled in brocade and plush.

Inevitably, these new ideals of simplicity, naturalness, and casualness were turned on architectural design, with the result that showy ornament and whimsical form became anathema. They served no practical purpose, it was charged. In Chicago, architects were introducing the intriguing new architectural theory "form follows function" into skyscraper design, and Bay Area architects and critics felt residence design should do no less.

Thus spoke the San Francisco plan book editor Alex F. Oakley: "An honestly built house on a well-arranged plan . . . must look like what it is — a comfortable place to live in." A writer for *California Architect and Engineer* emphatically agreed: "In planning a home the thought should be uppermost that use and beauty are to be everywhere wedded into the composition . . . The simpler, the more rational the plan, the more beautiful it becomes . . . The controlling thought in house-building should be simplicity and genuineness." And he hadn't a doubt in the world that the rational, genuine, beautiful line was the straight, chaste, unadorned one.

Simplicity equals beauty! Less is more! This strange new idea was fascinating — and contagious. Soon a club had formed in Berkeley dedicated to that creed. It was composed of architects,

Ernest Coxhead, an Englishman transplanted to Berkeley in the 1890s, designed some distinguished shingled houses reminiscent of English cottages. This house built in 1892 for William E. Loy on Ellsworth Street was noted for its simplicity and for its tasteful detailing, both inside and out. It had a charming side entrance tucked under an overhang. *(Architectural Documents Collection, College of Environmental Design, University of California)*

writers, artists and mere aesthetes, and they called themselves the Hillside Club. At first it was their modest aim to encourage simple, tasteful residences in the craggy hill district north of the University of California campus. Members offered to donate their not inconsiderable talents to "anyone who may apply for cooperation in the matter of planning a home or garden." Many gratefully accepted, then joined the club.

It was Hillsider credo that ideally all of the houses on a block should harmonize. Numerous home-builders respectfully submitted to such harmony under the Hillsiders' guidance. While preferring straight-lined houses, the club liked its streets convoluted and set itself up as watchdog over the city and real estate developers to ensure delightful contours. Club members were dedicated tree preservers and tree planters. They also went in for handicrafts, such as pottery, leather work, and furniture making, so that after a member had fashioned a perfect house he might then perfect its decor.

With their ideas catching on — or, at least, being discussed — all over the Bay Area, members began to widen their scope. They envisioned spreading their message across the land, and as a starter composed a letter and mailed it out broadside over the state suggesting that its recipients formulate a "plan of co-operation for architectural improvement of the cities and towns of California." It rather imperiously requested them to "form a section for studying the art of making homes beautiful, without and within, through simple means, and then aiding to carry out this idea in home building in your community."

No scholar has ever come forth to measure the precise radius of influence of the Hillside Club (which is still going strong, although its function today is mainly social), but the answer to these and other clarion calls for housing plain and uncorrupted was the bungalow. Although its name derived from *bengali*, which referred to the low thatched houses that evolved from the platformed service tents in which the British Army quartered

BIRTHDAY·FESTIVAL·IN·HONOR·OF·THE·ROYAL·CHILD·KI·
YIPPI·KI·YI·HELD·AT·THE·IMPERIAL·PARK·NAN·YUAN·
OF·THE·SUMMER·PALACE·WITH·DEMONSTRATIONS·
APPROPRIATE·TO·THE·COMPLETION·OF·THE·FOURTH·YEAR·
:·OF·:·HIS·AGE·:·
··:·:·:·:··

The straw-hatted and flower-bonneted throng are enjoying the University of California's Senior Class Day Pageant in Ben Weed's Amphitheater in the campus eucalyptus grove in the spring of 1898. They were treated to an unusual original production with an indeterminate Oriental setting. The playbill, whose heading appears at left, was pen-lettered on a long Chinese red scroll. Listed were such characters as Warden of the Imperial Dungeons, Lily Foot Ladies, Bearer of the Rice Bowl, Leader of the Kotow, Buddhist Missionaries to America, Tea Tasters, Samplers of Gin Seng, and Envoy Extraordinary Bearing Special Advices from the President of the University of California. The audience appears rapt. The outdoor theater, scene of many popular gatherings, was named for the student who discovered the remarkable acoustical properties of the hollow in the campus hills. Some years later, at the suggestion of President Benjamin Ide Wheeler and through the financing of William Randolph Hearst, it became the site of the Greek Theater. (*Berkeley Firefighters Association*)

The old Key Route Inn, which stood at Oakland's Broadway and Twenty-second Street (now Grand Avenue), was the pulsing center of the busy Key Route network of electric interurban lines. Every twenty minutes a train departed from the ground-level tunnel and clanged off for the Key Route pier; enroute to San Francisco. The Inn was also a transfer point for local streetcars. The Tudor-style building was the design of Edward T. Foulkes, who came to Oakland in 1893 after graduating from the Massachusetts Institute of Technology. Foulkes also designed the Tribune Tower and the Bishop Playhouse that became the Fulton and Franklin Theaters in its latter days. (*North collection*)

in India, this stocky residence style with the appeal of a wholesome country girl was spawned in California. It issued in the mid-1890s, a surprising mating of the Spanish adobe house and the New England cottage. The architectural historian Harold Kirker believes that a design by A. W. Putnam in the November, 1888 *California Architect and Building News* was probably its earliest precursor.

This whimsical account of its origin was offered in 1906 by Una Nixon Hopkins in *California*

Architect and Engineer: "Some independent soul bought an out-of-the-way plot of ground, built a low-rambling house in keeping with the location, made it in color to harmonize with the grass, the trees, the flowers — called it a bungalow, and lo! A new era of home-making was upon us." Miss Hopkins noted that bungalows were especially favored by "artistic people."

The bungalow was simple. Typically, it was a one-story, box-like dwelling, topped with a shallow gable roof with overhanging eaves and fronted

It was in the East Bay hills that Louis Christian Mullgardt designed his first California houses — low, simple bungalows of natural materials, whose rooms were stepped along gradient foundations. His first California design to reach construction was this 1907 house at 43 Dormidera Avenue in Piedmont, now the home of Attorney Thomas B. Swartz. Its exterior is rough-sawn redwood clapboards, Mullgardt's favorite building material for his early houses. *(Architectural Documents Collection, College of Environmental Design, University of California)*

with a wide, open porch supported by posts or pillars made of cement or stone boulders. Like the Indian tent, it squatted square on raised foundations.

And it was natural. Bungalow builders made a point of using indigenous materials — redwood, pine, field stone and cement — and leaving them crudely unfinished. It was felt that paint and varnish spoiled wood, which was preferred in its natural state. If color was imperative, then a light stain might be applied, but it should be of a hue suggested by nature. Untreated shingles or board and batten were the usual exterior cover. Stucco was permissible for exteriors "so long as it is used over wood confessedly as stucco." The same held for interior plaster, which if chosen "must be rough and used in connection with plenty of wood."

Ornament was eschewed unless it "grew out of construction." Out went machine-turned molding, sawed-out bracketry, and other fussy millwork. A magazine writer reviewing one East Bay house approvingly noted the "grateful absence of moldings; one realizes also that he has not seen a planed or molded stick of wood in the outside construction." It was felt that all the ornament one needed was abundant in the natural beauties of the garden, visible through the big sashed windows, forerunner of the modern picture window.

Certainly, the bungalow was casual. Gone were both entrance hall and the long central hall. The front door opened without fanfare into the living room, which opened without so much as a door into the dining room. Many bungalows had, as well, what was termed "an intimate asso-

One of the few examples of the work of the Green brothers of Pasadena outside their home territory is this fine house at 2307 Piedmont Avenue that today houses Sigma Phi fraternity. Although built unstintingly for a banker, the house was called a bungalow, a term used more loosely then than today. Narrow stairs lead from both sides of the property line up to the front entrance. Splendid details are the wrought iron gates and the stained art glass of the front door. (*T. W. Tenney*)

The late Victorian Era saw a revival of Tudor, a Sixteenth Century English secular style, which used Gothic pointed forms, but substituted brick and half-timber for stone. In California, Tudor underwent still another translation with shingles being substituted for brick. This circa Tudor house, which stood at 2045 Central Avenue in Alameda, was the early home of Dr. George P. Reynolds and was later occupied by Dr. Omer R. Etter. The mullioned windows are a true Tudor feature. (*Alameda Historical Society*)

The rim of Lake Merritt was undergoing a transformation with bungalows and paved thoroughfares to accommodate the invading automobile when this photograph was made in 1922. Remaining, however, were a few of the magnificent live oaks that once shaded the district. The camera was looking up Lakeshore Avenue from Stowe Avenue. (*Albert Norman collection*)

A familiar landmark on the Berkeley skyline is the baroque cupola of the Berkeley City Hall, erected in 1908. (*Albert Norman collection*)

159

On a dry October day in 1901, fire enveloped the Ballard residence, a rambling Queen Anne. On its site in 1914 rose the elegant Claremont Hotel, below, which architect Frank Lloyd Wright once called "one of the few hotels in the world with warmth, character, and charm." Klondike millionaire Erick Lindblom built the Mediterranean style hotel to be a fitting resort for visiting millionaires from the East and from Europe. They did not come in sufficient numbers, and the hotel began changing hands, coming into the ownership of realtor Frank Havens, who reputedly won it in a checker game with "Borax" Smith. Thereafter, the hotel's fortunes began waxing and it was to enjoy a peak of success during the 1930s, when it was a fashionable social center and nightly offered ballroom dancing to big name bands. *(Louis Stein and Cliff Bond)*

Warm and hospitable in its mood is Julia Morgan's six-story Berkeley City Club at 2315 Durant Avenue, a Mediterranean-style building that has reminders of San Simeon. While eclectic in derivation, the design is highly functional in that its splendid features supply form and decoration without extraneous appendages. Concrete is used frankly, and beams and vaulting are structural necessities.

Besides the forty-two hotel rooms and suites, the club has a drawing room, lounge rooms, an auditorium, and an Olympic-size swimming pool. Among many opulent interior details are four decorative fireplaces, wood paneling embellished with hand-carved medallions, and colored tile floors. (*T. W. Tenney*)

ciation with nature," this being an uncovered side or back porch that served as an outdoor living room, first cousin to today's patio. So close in spirit was the casual bungalow to the modern ranch style house that a half century later Russell Lynes would describe the latter as being "a bungalow pulled out like a piece of taffy and bent."

Whether the bungalow first saw light in Northern or Southern California remains moot; architectural scholars are unable to agree on whether the chief contributions to the style were made by Bay Area or Los Angeles architects. Most who argue the former will cite as their two chief reasons Bernard Maybeck and Julia Morgan. Certainly,

these extraordinarily talented architects took the bungalow and made of it something much greater.

This pair had in common a Beaux-Arts education, mastery of detail, a preference for principle over style, a prodigious output, and long life (both died in 1957). They were good friends, sometimes collaborators, and each admired the other. Both enjoyed commercial success (though hers was greater) and top professional honors. Both helped change the course of architectural history.

There the similarity ends. In both their professional and personal habits they couldn't have been more different. She was brisk, businesslike, systematic, possessed of executive ability with

Julia Morgan

Bernard Maybeck

which she presided with authority over a large staff in an impressive suite of offices in San Francisco's Merchants Exchange building; he had a purely artistic nature, was erratic, temperamental, unconcerned with money, worked mostly alone, preferring his drawing board set up under an oak tree. Her preliminary sketches for clients were immaculately precise, explicit with sizes and specifications; his resembled the sketches of a poet on holiday, with a hint of a building shrouded in foliage and reflected in a mirror lake. She was indifferent about food and rest, often worked marathon stretches on black coffee; he was a health addict, with an exhaustive list of food taboos. She dressed impeccably, preferring well-tailored suits and imported silk blouses; he, in addition to affecting a spectacular beard, was the most peculiar dresser known to Berkeley in its pre-hippie days, wearing a wardrobe of his own whimsical design that included a knit beret and voluminous, side-fastening trousers that reached to his armpits. In sum, she was an arch conservative, he the Bay Area's best known eccentric.

Maybeck had scarcely any experience when he arrived in San Francisco in 1889. Of Swiss ancestry, he had grown up in New York's Greenwich Village, where his father plied the woodcarving trade. After returning from architecture study at the Beaux-Arts in Paris, he worked briefly in Florida, then went to Kansas City and opened an office. But he didn't get any business, so he decided to try his luck in California.

In San Francisco, he went to work in the office of A. Page Brown, where he promptly characterized himself as both independent and romantic by using a lady love's initials as the motif in a terra cotta frieze on the downtown Crocker Building that he helped design. But Maybeck's work pleased his client, as did virtually everything he executed during his exuberant career.

As newcomer Willis Polk had been captivated by the missions, Maybeck was intrigued and inspired by California redwood — by its color, breadth and workability. He couldn't wait to start experimenting with it. Establishing his home in Berkeley, where he had been asked to teach a

This redwood shingle house with its rustic simplicity and chalet features is characteristic of many of Bernard Maybeck's early residential designs. He was both architect and contractor for this 1906 house at 1326 Arch Street for which John McLaren, long-time superintendent of Golden Gate Park, designed the formal garden. Another Maybeck trademark is the great brick fireplace with wrought-iron-trimmed cabinets that fills one end of the high-ceilinged living room. The house is now the John H. Quinn residence. Mrs. Quinn is Theodora Kroeber, the author of *Ishi in Two Worlds.* (T. W. Tenney)

course in descriptive geometry at the University, he was fascinated with the community's casual life style and with the town's tilted terrain. He undertook to incorporate the three elements — redwood, casualness and hilliness — into architecture. He soon had scope for experimentation in commissions to build homes for fellow faculty members and for members of the Hillside Club.

Accepting the challenge of building on the slant, even on the most precipitous "goat lot," Maybeck delighted in making houses "climb the hill." Working in redwood, he employed simple post and beam construction, fashioning squared-off houses with shallow gable roofs and shingled sides. Often he left his construction unashamedly evident, even accentuated it. Sometimes he constructed a house wrong-side-out with the studding on the exterior; inside naked joists and beams were frankly visible.

His houses not only dispensed with the central hall, but in some of them one long room did double duty as living room and dining room. In the Berkeley house at 23 Panoramic Way today called "The Chalet," designed for a University professor, he made the combination living room-dining room into an L-shape. John Entenza, editor of *Arts and Architecture,* said, "When the wall separating dining room from living room was removed, all Berkeley was shocked." Berkeley did, however, come around to accepting it, but so far as is known Maybeck found no takers for his inspiration of combining the living room and the kitchen, where he said "dish washing could become a pleasant social pastime." That notion was, of course, a half century ahead of its time.

This trend toward room combining was a revolt against the rigid room separation and compartmenting of the Victorian Era. The architecture magazines termed it "open planning" and said it accomplished "an informal flow of space from one room to another." Man or breeze could wander unobstructed through the open portals, through rooms uncluttered by molding, carpet or drapery. This minimum of dust-catching elements permitted a welcomed minimum of maintenance in a decade when female domestic servants were beginning to defect to attend business schools and learn the mysteries of the typewriter.

While retaining the fundamental simplicity of the bungalow—the shallow gable roof and rectangular ground plan—Maybeck soon was modifying the style. On his drawing board, residence design never stood still. He gave the bungalow an upstairs by pitching the roof steeper, fitting another floor under it, and admitting light with dormers. In some of these early commissions, he incorporated modified Japanese and Swiss chalet elements that were widely copied by bungalow builders.

The house he built for Guy Hyde Chick at 7133 Chabot Road in Oakland, in addition to being one of his most charming designs, is a veritable museum of Maybeck innovations. A striking feature of this combination board and batten, shingle, and concrete design is the cantilevered gable, which extends two feet beyond the first floor. Upstairs closets were likewise thrust out over a side wall, providing interesting overhangs. In the Chick living room, he grouped floor-to-ceiling windows and French doors, in effect creating glass walls.

He liked to employ large projecting beams, and sometimes, as in The Chalet, he pushed trusses through the roof to meet beams thrust through the eaves, a scheme as decorative as it was practical. He liked verticality, and his designs grew higher and higher. As one of his carpenters put it, "He liked plenty of room up there." His fireplaces, which had started out quite small, ended up being walk-in-size.

His interior designs were equally inventive. He was ahead of his time in infusing interiors with natural light, often employing clerestories, groups of windows placed at the peak of the gable, that flooded living rooms with dramatic beams of light. In the Chick residence he introduced indirect lighting recessed in ceiling coves. To provide contrast, the ceiling was varied from seven to eleven feet. In several of his early houses, he divided the main downstairs rooms with sliding doors (another Japanese touch), which might be flung open to create one large moving space. He made ample use of built-in furniture, such as bookcases, cabinets and wall seats.

After the 1923 fire destroyed many of his residences in north Berkeley, Maybeck began to develop a style in stucco and tile and thereafter built only semi-fireproof residences in that district. One of his finest examples was this house for the Kennedy family at Euclid Avenue and Buena Vista Way. The house is important both for its plastic form (note curved street-front walls and ramp) and for its unique color scheme. Experimenting with ways to "age" stucco walls, he colored the walls in tones graduating from soft peach to burnt orange, using the darker tones up under the eaves. The design also incorporates his favorite Gothic ornament and his familiar split gable roof. (T. W. Tenney)

Gentility was wed to the vernacular in Bernard Maybeck's First Church of Christ Scientist in Berkeley, and the result was this simple, yet elegant design. In this world-famous church he successfully mingled such historic elements as Gothic tracery and Romanesque columns, the bungalow's shallow gables and low spread, and the factory's sash windows and asbestos siding. He summed up his intent as "a church that would look like a church" and be built of materials "that are what they claim to be, not imitations."
(T. W. Tenney)

Also highly imaginative was his treatment of materials. He lightly charred the surface of roughly-sawn timber to provide a soft, wavy texture and treated redwood with sulphate of iron to lend a silvery tint. He amazed his contractors by employing a washing machine to concoct a unique variety of porous cement, which he called "bubble stone." He built a house for himself at 2701 Buena Vista Way composed of giant shingles made by dipping burlap sacks in the mixture and hanging them on wire mesh. In his Palace of Fine Arts, built for the Panama-Pacific International Exposition of 1915 (restored in the 1960s), he made extensive use of a new material called "staff," a mixture of plaster and burlap-type fiber. In his most famous design — that is also his most lyrical — the First Church of Christ Scientist in Berkeley, he blithely commingled redwood, reinforced concrete, steel trusses, asbestos siding, and factory sash windows! Built in 1910, today it is one of the most admired church buildings in America.

Berkeley's Town and Gown Club, built in 1901 and still in use, combines the charm of Maybeck's early shingled houses with dramatic structural features. The exterior is an open book in which the structural plan can be read. Upon entering the lower floor one has the feeling of entering an arc, this suggested by the imaginative use of V-bracing. The upstairs auditorium was built by Julia Morgan, and in the 1940s its huge oriental lanterns were replaced by more modern lighting designed by architect Robert Ratcliff.

Maybeck's work during those formative years must have been exciting to watch. It still has the capacity to excite. And, of course, the master's dazzling inventiveness never flagged during his career that spanned seven decades. In 1951, the man who came West because he lacked commissions, was awarded the American Institute of Architects gold medal of achievement. Only three other men had received it.

The bungalow already had been introduced by the time Julia Morgan arrived in the East Bay, in 1902. Arrived back, that is. The daughter of a pioneer Oakland family, she had grown up in a big Stick-Eastlake house at Fourteenth and Brush Streets, but had spent the last eight years in Paris at the Beaux-Arts. When she enrolled there they had informed her that, being a woman, she wouldn't, of course, be awarded a diploma. They probably wondered who in the world would hire a woman architect, especially one trained in institutional architecture. They were as yet unacquainted with the mettle of Julia, who as a child had risked workouts on her brother's gymnastic equipment (punishment was extra violin practice), and, later, had braved resentful stares of male college students in order to win an engineering degree at the University.

They became acquainted with it. When at the end of her Beaux-Arts course of study, her degree was withheld, Julia re-enrolled in the school and worked part time for a Paris architect. By winning every school competition she was eligible to enter, she embarrassed the authorities into granting her degree — the first Beaux-Arts degree in architecture ever awarded a woman.

Returned with her hard-earned degree in her pocket, she went to work for John Galen Howard, a Massachusetts native who had come out to be supervising architect at the University. She assisted Howard in the designs of several early campus buildings, including the Hearst Memorial Mining Building and the Greek Theater. It was her talented work on the former building that brought her to the attention of Mrs. Phoebe Hearst, who had endowed the building in memory of her husband, the late senator. Mrs. Hearst's admiration for the budding young architect led to the commission to design the aforementioned Hacienda, which in turn opened other important doors.

By 1905, Julia Morgan had her own office in San Francisco and a waiting clientele. Her solid grounding in the classics won her the commission to rebuild the fire-gutted Fairmont Hotel after the earthquake. The earthquake brought so much public and institutional work to her office that she had to advertise all over the world for the draftsmen she needed.

While moving with assurance between these widely varied commissions and motifs, she had still another iron in the fire. A great volume of residence designs was flowing from her drawing board. She quickly caught the knack of the low, boxy shingle houses with interior flow that were rising in the East Bay foothills. Soon she was adding massing ideas and details of her own — less whimsical than those of the dreamy Maybeck, but just as pleasing in their own way. Many of her commissions were for University professors and for Oakland and Piedmont businessmen.

Increasingly her residences partook of her individuality, acquiring certain qualities that stamped them a "Julia Morgan house." One of these was original and flawless detailing, for to her the minute touches were as important as the broad concept. Although she made use of derivative material, it served as an impetus rather than a direct motif. The eye-pleasing details on her residences — the delightful windows, doors, staircases, mantlepieces — were wholly hers in character and always appropriate for the house. The entrances she designed for the Charles B. Wells residence in the Rockridge district of Oakland and for the E. W. Linforth house on Berkeley's Derby Street are works of haunting loveliness.

These stunning yet muted effects were painstakingly arrived at. From everyone who worked with her comes the word "perfectionist." This quiet woman who never married and for whom architecture was her life accepted nothing but the best, whether from herself or from those in her employ. Retired Oakland architect Louis Schalk, who worked in her office, says that after each commission was completed, she called in her staff and invited their opinions as to how the house or building might have been constructed better. While gratefully accepting criticism, she unhesitatingly gave it. She often picked up a tool from a craftsman and, demonstrating, said, "Do it this way, Friend." She climbed flimsy and lofty scaffolding to inspect work at close hand. She was known to have work ripped out that did not meet her standards. Yet both professionals and craftsmen vied to work for her, for what they could learn and for the sincere appreciation good work received.

Likewise, all materials she used were carefully selected, and, when delivered, examined with a captious eye. Mrs. Mary Tusher, Oakland YWCA administrator, recalls that when Julia Morgan was building the 1914 Oakland YWCA, whose exterior design includes fifty tile columns that flank the upper windows, the tiny woman sat down and lifted in turn thousands of pieces of tile, focusing intently on each piece through her gold-rimmed glasses. All imperfect tile was returned to the supplier.

Another Morgan strong point was interior organization. Her conveniently-organized floor plans made for maximum circulation. While avoiding the long hallway, she made it possible to enter rooms without having to pass through others. She often accomplished this feat by placing the entrance at the center of one side and opening into a small square hall. Her planning thus was from the inside out.

This side entrance was a feature of the charming two-story shingle house she built on Berkeley's upper Durant Avenue for Miss Lucy Stebbins, dean of women at the University. Regretably demolished to make way for a swimming pool was the somewhat similarly-planned house that she built in 1909 on Berkeley's Prospect Street for her younger sister Emma (also a tradition-breaker, she studied for the law). This excellently-proportioned, two-story shingle with the bungalow's low-pitched gable roof was representative of her early houses.

Also remaining from those years are two shingle houses that stand at 2814 and 2816 Derby Street in Berkeley. Especially handsome is the window treatment of these houses, which are uniquely arranged to face each other at right angles. They were built respectively in 1906 and 1910, the house of the latter date being occupied by Thaddeus Joy, an architect in her office who assisted on these designs; Joy's widow still resides there.

Julia Morgan went on to design more than two thousand buildings, public and private, in California, Utah, Hawaii and Japan, and, as all the world knows, was the architect for William Randolph Hearst's fabulous San Simeon castle overlooking the Pacific Ocean (since 1958 a California state park). San Simeon has a Berkeley echo in her magnificent six-story Women's City Club, which was the only completed building of a planned complex of three. At the height of her career she had her own plane and pilot to check on her broad sphere of operation. Such were her accomplishments, she was widely called the world's greatest woman architect, and the University of California bestowed upon her its highest award, an honorary doctorate of laws degree.

Yet, one of her finest statements remains a simple frame church she built in Berkeley during her early period. St. John's Presbyterian Church on College Avenue with its simple post and beam construction and shallow gables has a dignity and integrity that survives, defying the rigors of time and fashion. This structure is wholly lacking in pretense. As a safeguard against fire, the framing of walls, trusses and posts was left open, but in her sensitive hands this practical scheme emerged as an arrestingly beautiful design. Such honest structural framing placed this modest church far ahead of its time. Like Maybeck's Christian Science church, St. John's is a must for visitors of an architectural bent. Both churches were built in 1909.

John Galen Howard, the University supervising architect and later its architecture professor, was another graduate of the Beaux-Arts who contributed to East Bay residence design. Although he is best known for his campus designs (which include Sather Tower, California Hall, The Library, and the old architecture school buildings), he did execute a number of residence commissions, most of which, along with scores of Morgan and Maybeck houses, were destroyed in 1923 by the disastrous fire in north Berkeley.

Among remaining Howard designs is the Gregory house, a long, low-slung frame house, which he built in 1908 in three stages — the prototype of the "growing house." Another is the wide-eaved frame house he built for himself in 1912, to which Julia Morgan later made additions. Howard's first Berkeley residence was a rambling post and beam design that combined roughly-dashed cement and redwood shakes. This much-admired house, which crowned a rise on Ridge Road, in 1907 was the subject of a full-length article, one of a series on homes of famous architects, published by the national magazine *Indoors and Out*.

In Southern California the chief innovators in bungalow design were the Pasadena Green brothers, Charles S. and Henry M. In 1908, Green and

A Berkeley design that may have primed Bernard Maybeck's inspiration for the Palace of Fine Arts is this residence at 2798 Buena Vista Way called "Temple of the Wings," formerly called "Temple of the Winds." He was asked to design a semicircular colonnaded loggia for Mrs. Florence Boynton, a dancing teacher who was a friend of Isadora Duncan and once was engaged to Isadora's brother, Augustine. But Maybeck and Mrs. Boynton disagreed over the number and closeness of the columns and severed their association. Mrs. Boynton modified the design to suit her preference, while Maybeck turned his attention to designing an art gallery for the Panama-Pacific International Exposition. It is said he was determined to demonstrate his mastery with columns. Both palace and residence (now occupied by Mrs. Boynton's daughter, Mrs. Sulgwynn Quitzow) are durable favorites with the public. *(Arthur Gough)*

Green, in one of their few professional ventures out of the Los Angeles area, invaded Maybeck and Morgan territory when commissioned by the San Francisco banker William Thorsen to design a home for him at 2307 Piedmont Avenue in Berkeley. In this fine example of their work, the designers anticipated the ranch house floor plan when they elongated their shingled, gabled, deep-eaved dwelling into an L-shape, although giving it two floors. Flush ceiling lights and electrically operated flush panel doors were among the advanced features of this residence, which today houses the Sigma Phi fraternity.

By 1909, according to *California Architect and Engineer*, the bungalow, "our special pride," had become "ubiquitous along the Pacific Coast." What's more the chunky airy style was sweeping the country, with bungalows popping up in New England, on the Midwestern prairie, along the Gulf Coast. California was now up on the big board in architecture, there to remain. Lewis Mumford has said that the bungalow and its complement Mission furniture were "the first designs that put California esthetically on the modern map," and in the view of Russell Lynes, "The bungalow probably had more to do with how suburban Americans live today than any other building that has gone even remotely by the name of architecture in our history."

While these bold experimenters, Maybeck, Morgan, and their followers, were striking a mighty blow against Victorian architecture, other East Bay graduates were in their quite different ways helping to write an end to the antimacassar era that shaped them. Bret Harte's stories took broadsides at Victorian prudishness, by celebrating the virtues of society's tarnished outcasts. Oakland schoolmaster Edwin Markham with his compelling poetry championed the liberation of the under-paid working class. His "Man With a Hoe" not only hurled him into a vortex of national eulogy, but branded a symbol of the common man upon a burgeoning social consciousness. And no book of the era did more to undermine laissez faire economics than did tax reform crusader Henry George's *Progress and Poverty,* which he wrote while working as an Oakland newspaper editor.

The proper pig-tailed little Stein girl with her nose in the approved volume of Wordsworth was to lead the plunge into experimental literature. Gertrude Stein quite merrily jettisoned every vestige of traditional literary form — plot, paragraph, sentence, punctuation; she even created her own esoteric vocabulary. Her childhood playmate Isadora Duncan, dancing on the most glittering stages of Europe dressed only in a chiffon veil, and sometimes discarding that, pioneered the revolutionary modern dance. If she didn't quite attain her goal of eclipsing the classical ballet, Isadora did wage effective side campaigns against the fetters of corsetry and in behalf of free love, joyful and unashamed.

But most critical of all of the precincts that molded him was Jack London, who drew a bead on the cultural and moral pretensions of the Victorian Era, on its myopic preoccupation with respectability and social convention — on all that so bedazzled the impressionable Martin Eden.

After toilfully lifting himself out of society's cellar, London became bitterly disillusioned with what he found in the drawing room. He pronounced gentility a hypocritical sham, as false as a theatrical backdrop, and he burned not only to expose it but to ring it down for good. The underlying message of his later writings was, "Go native, young man — don't be beguiled by the trappings of culture." His recurrent theme was to contrast civilization with primitive society, or with the law of the wolf pack, with civilization coming off a shoddy second best. When literary success suddenly made him world famous and a millionaire, and the elite of Oakland were vying for his company, London might have built himself the finest house in the East Bay and lorded it over what he once had groveled before. Instead, heaping imprecation upon urban society, he retreated to a ranch in Sonoma County's lonely Valley of the Moon.

The Victorian Era was reversed — its morals, its culture, its design. Most of all, its architecture was scornfully rejected. Those carefully-wrought forms, that once proud ornament that had given pleasure and conferred status throughout the romantic decades now were roundly condemned as dishonest, even immoral. They became not merely declassé but disgraced. They stood accused of not serving practicality, and of pretending to something they were not. Gothic had pointed toward a heaven it no longer remembered. The Italian Villa had given itself the airs of past Renaissance grandeur. Southern Colonial had faked chivalry, as Mission had asceticism and piety. All of this, it now seemed, had been foolish fancy, and so was to be thrust aside, rejected like fairy tales that once had delighted but now were said to have denied reality and taught the wrong lessons.

And so the modern "functional" house prevailed. New dogma pronounced the straight line to be more lovely than the curve, and we were given houses that were simple, square and sterile — houses that were housing, housing that sometimes was merely shelter. Modern functionalism went far beyond what beauty-loving Bernard Maybeck and Julia Morgan had in mind. Maybeck, when asked his opinion of modern residential design, would shrug and ask, "You mean all those boxes?" Once when pressed to expand, he characterized them as "unlovely structures designed for holding machines."

Popularly known as "The Castle," this house that saddles the crest of the north Berkeley hills at 2900 Buena Vista Way, derived its inspiration from French ecclesiastical architecture of the transition period between Romanesque and Gothic. Its most outstanding architectural feature is a cloister, replica of one originally built in Toulouse, France, and now in a museum.

The house was built in the 1920s by the late Samuel J. Hume, who directed the Greek Theater and was owner of the "Sign of the Palindrome," a store specializing in imported books that was a gathering place for the literati. It remains the home of his widow Dr. Portia Bell Hume, a psychiatrist and sculptress. "The Castle" was one of the few eclectic designs of John Hudson Thomas. Although the house has only one story, its rooms rest on four different levels. Many of the rooms are furnished with Gothic furniture. See living room at right.
(*Oakland* TRIBUNE)

Maybeck's comments recall the words of another Berkeley resident, the song-writer Malvina Reynolds, who had her definitive say on tract development housing:

"Little boxes on the hillside,
  Little boxes made of ticky tacky,
Little boxes on the hillside,
  Little boxes all the same.
There's a green one and a pink one,
  And a blue one and a yellow one,
And they're all made out of ticky tacky,
  And they all look just the same." *

Now the pendulum is swinging back again. Victorian values are being reassessed, and the discovery has been made that the era of flickering gaslight and pestilent drains was a time of bold and courageous striving, what's more of immense achievement. It was also an era of warmth and enthusiasm, of passion and splendor. It is this new reassessment, of course, that underlies the current enthusiastic revival of Victorian objects and design.

Architects, ever sensitive to the public temper, are quite aware of this change of heart. Just as they were responsive to the mood of casualness and practicality, today they are sensitive to these new vibrations, which are trickling onto their drawing boards. They have perceived that man who not long ago preferred his domicile immaculately unadorned today has begun to feel bereft without a touch of ornament. Thus we note a return to decorative building screens, of incised and molded design, of curvilinear detail. By the same token, shingles are back, so are balconies and bay windows. Large kitchens are in vogue again, as are high ceilings. Privacy-lovers, surfeited with "togetherness" and rooms that "flow into each other," are demanding more room separation. There's even a return to the second parlor, although called by other names.

In short, we are making the discovery that Victorian houses were functional, after all — that is, if we take the word at its literal meaning of something that "serves," something that prompts "the kind of activity proper to a person." For we don't any of us live by practicality alone, but equally by beauty, stimulus, and imagination — all qualities possessed in abundance by those eye-pleasing, private, roomy, airy houses we call Victorians.

Bibliography

Edson, F. Adams, *Oakland's Early History*, Oakland, Calif., 1932.

Julia Cooley Altrocchi, *The Spectacular San Franciscans*, New York, E. P. Dutton, 1949.

American Heritage Publishing Co., Inc., New York, *The Pioneer Spirit*, 1959.

Joseph A. Baird, *Time's Wondrous Changes*, San Francisco, California Historical Society, 1962.

Lucius Beebe and Charles Clegg, *San Francisco's Golden Era*, Berkeley, Calif., Howell-North Books, 1960.

Carl Bode, *The Anatomy of American Popular Culture*, Berkeley, Calif., University of California Press, 1959.

George T. Bromley, *The Long Ago and the Later On*, San Francisco, A. M. Robertson, 1904.

John Burchard and Albert Bush-Brown, *The Architecture of America, A Social and Cultural History*, Boston, Little, Brown, 1961.

Mary Cable, *Dream Castles*, Viking, 1966.

Mary Cable, *American Manners and Morals*, New York, American Heritage Publishing Co., 1969.

Kenneth Cardwell and William C. Hays, "Fifty Years from Now," *California Monthly*, April, 1954.

John Walton Caughey, *California*, Prentice-Hall, 1953.

Helen Comstock, *American Furniture*, New York, Viking Press, 1962.

G. A. Cummings and E. S. Bladwell, *Oakland — A History*, published by the Grant D. Miller Mortuaries, Inc., 1942.

William Heath Davis, *75 Years in California*, San Francisco, John Howell, 1929.

Daisy De Veer, *The Story of Rancho Antonio*, Oakland, 1924.

W. W. Elliott, *Oakland and Surroundings Illustrated and Described*, Oakland, 1885.

James Marston Fitch, *American Building*, Boston, Houghton, Mifflin, 1948.

Merrill Folsom, *More Great American Mansions and Their Stories*. New York, Hastings House, 1967.

Porter Garnett, *Stately Homes of California*, Boston, Little, Brown, 1915.

Curt Gentry, *San Francisco and the Bay Area*, New York, Doubleday, 1962.

George Grotz, *The New Antiques*, Garden City, New York, Doubleday, 1964.

William Halley, *The Centennial Year Book of Alameda County*, Oakland, 1876.

Mary R. Houston, "The Early History of Berkeley," M. A. Thesis, University of California, 1925.

Heribert Hutter, *Art Nouveau*, New York, Crown, 1965.

H. W. Janson, *History of Art*, Prentice-Hall, 1967.

Mary Johnson, *The City of Berkeley*, Oakland, 1942.

Robert Furneaux Jordan, *Victorian Architecture*, Pelican Books, 1968.

Charles Augustus Keeler, *The Simple Home*, San Francisco, Paul Elder, 1904.

Harold Kirker, *California's Architectural Frontier*, San Marino, Calif., Huntington Library, 1960.

Harold Kirker, "California Architecture in the Nineteenth Century: A Social History," Ph.D. Thesis, University of California, Berkeley, June, 1957.

Oscar Lewis, *Here Lived the Californians*, New York, Rinehart, 1957.

Frances Lichten, *Decorative Art of Victoria's Era*, Charles Scribner's, 1950.

Life Magazine Publishing Co., *The Fabulous Century*, Vol. 1, 1970.

Sarah M. Lockwood, *Decoration — Past, Present and Future*, Garden City, New York, Doubleday, Doran, 1934.

Jack London, *Martin Eden*, Baltimore, Md., Penguin, 1967.

Russell Lynes, "The Age of Taste," *Harper's Magazine*, October, 1950.

Russell Lynes, *The Tastemakers*, New York, Harper and Brothers, 1954.

Russell Lynes, *The Domesticated Americans*, Harper and Row, 1963.

John Maass, *The Gingerbread Age*, New York, Rinehart, 1957.

Edwin Markham, *California the Wonderful*, Hearst's International Library Co., 1914.

Katharine M. McClinton, *Collecting American Victorian Antiques*, Charles Scribner's, 1950.

Esther McCoy, *Five California Architects*, New York, Reinhold, 1960.

Frank C. Merritt, *History of Alameda County*, Chicago, Clark Publishing Co., 2 vols., 1928.

Lewis Mumford, *The Brown Decades*, New York, Dover, 1955.

Lewis Mumford, *Roots of American Architecture*, Evergreen, 1958.

Lewis Mumford, *The City in History*, New York, Harcourt, Brace & World, 1961.

Amelia Ransome Neville, *The Fantastic City: Memoirs of the Social and Romantic Life of Old San Francisco*, Boston, Houghton Mifflin, 1932.

Ruth Newhall, *San Francisco's Enchanted Palace*, Berkeley, Calif., Howell-North Books, 1967.

Flora D. North, "She Built for the Ages," *Kappa Alpha Theta Journal*, Spring, 1967.

Alexander F. Oakey, *My House Is My Castle*, San Francisco, Pacific States Savings, Loan and Building Company, 1891.

The Pacific Tourist, New York, Crown, 1884.

Olive H. Palmer, *Vignettes of Early San Francisco Homes and Gardens*, San Francisco, 1935.

Marion R. Parsons, *Old California Houses: Portraits and Stories*, Berkeley, Calif., University of California Press, 1952.

Evelyn Craig Pattiani, *Queen of the Hills*, Fresno, Academy Library Guild, 1953.

J. H. Plumb, "The Victorians Unbuttoned," *Horizon*, Autumn, 1969.

Elinor Richey, "Kenwood Foils the Block-busters," *Harper's*, August, 1963.

Elinor Richey, "Crisis in Chicago," *American Literature Themes and Writers*, McGraw-Hill, 1967.

Ishbel Ross, *Taste in America*, Crowell, 1967.

Vincent J. Scully, *The Shingle Style*, New Haven, Conn., Yale University Press, 1955.

Isobel Field Strong, *This Life I've Loved*, New York and Toronto, Longmans, Green, 1937.

Thomas E. Tallmadge, *The Story of Architecture in America*, New York, W. J. Norton, 1927.

Christopher Tunnard with Henry Hope Reed, *American Skyline*, Boston, Houghton Mifflin, 1955.

Wesley D. Vail, *Victorians, An Account of Domestic Architecture in Victorian San Francisco*, San Francisco, 1964.

Franklin Walker, *San Francisco's Literary Frontier*, New York, A. A. Knopf, 1939.

Myron W. Wood, *The History of Alameda County, California, Including Its Geology, Topography, Soil, and Production*, Oakland, 1883.

John and Sally Woodbridge, *Buildings of the Bay Area*, New York, Grove Press, 1960.

Index